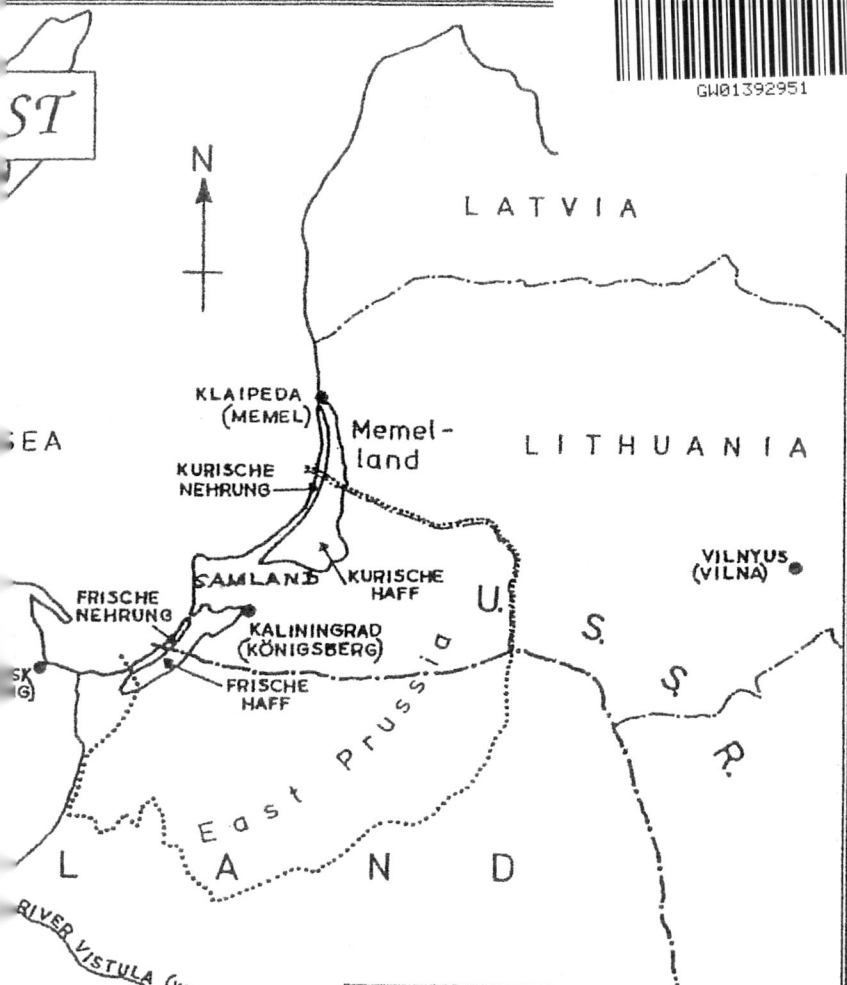

ST

N

LATVIA

SEA

KLAIPEDA
(MEMEL)

Memel-
land

LITHUANIA

KURISCHE
NEHRUNG

VILNYUS
(VILNA)

SAMLAND

KURISCHE
HAFF

U.

FRISCHE
NEHRUNG

S.

KALININGRAD
(KÖNIGSBERG)

East Prussia

S.

SK
G)

FRISCHE
HAFF

R.

L

A

N

D

RIVER VISTULA (WEICHSEL)

WARSZAWA

KEY

● TOWNS —
(PRE-1945 PLACENAMES
IN BRACKETS)

▬·—·▬ POST-WAR FRONTIERS

········· PRE-1945 GERMAN FRONTIER

GW01392951

BOUNCING BACK

MY AUTOBIOGRAPHY

JUTTA TYLER

PUBLISHED 2013

© Copyright 2013

ISBN: 978-0-9927437-0-3

Published by: Jutta Tyler
              81 Maritime Drive
              Carrickfergus
              Co. Antrim
              BT38 8GQ

Printed by: Browne Printers Ltd
              Port Road,
              Letterkenny.
              Co. Donegal
              Tel: (074) 9121387

Front cover: The author at the age of 12 and 20

I dedicate this work
to my family

I have deliberately disguised the identity of some of the individuals in this book. If I have left out anything, then either those events have become too blurred through the passing of time, or they are labelled 'strictly private' in the store-room of my mind. For any short-comings I sincerely apologise.

I also apologise for any inaccuracies in using reported speech. It would be impossible to be word-perfect after all those years without having had a tape recorder available at all times. I think, however, I have expressed the meaning of the facts and words fairly accurately.

I am indebted to my family for guidance, advice and proof-reading and I sincerely thank them.

I want to thank all my friends as well who encouraged me to write this book and there are many of them, from old established friends in Leatbeg, Castledawson and Heidelberg to not quite such long standing friends in Lissahully and Kinlough and to newly acquired ones in Freinsheim and Carrickfergus.

PART ONE

(A CHILD GROWS UP IN HITLER'S GERMANY)

PROLOGUE

We discovered more details about our distant relatives when my father was asked to supply his employer with certified documents of our family tree, dating back four generations. It was Hitler's idea of checking Jewish infiltration into the Aryan race.

My father's ancestors were all seafarers and had for generations lived in the Baltic port of Memel which, before 1945, was German. The eldest son was always called *John*. The surname was *Schiel* as was my maiden name. Both *John* and *Schiel* were not German names in those days. Now, with families having moved in all directions within Germany, the name *Schiel* can occasionally be found anywhere, but the computer records it as *North German*. To learn more about the first *John Schiel* we had to go back two further generations. The records revealed that yet another *Seemann John Schiel* had lived and died in Memel, but his country of origin and date of birth were not known, only his date of death. Sadly I have forgotten this potentially important date.

The authorities merely suggested that such incomplete records were those of a foreigner. We nicknamed him: John the First, wherever he came from.

I remember my father visiting relatives in Memel when I was very small. He had brought back a picture for my mother and a toy for me and told me about the endless forests of very tall trees which grew round the town of Memel and beyond. "If ever a child was lost in those forests it would never find its way home again," he told me. I was pleased I had not gone with him and was really not interested, but my father continued. "When the trees were tall enough they were cut down, they had their branches cut off and were rolled into the river. From there they floated to the harbour and got loaded into big boats to be sold." I tried to work that one out. "Why did people want to buy trees when they had so many already?" I was supposed to have asked. My father always knew an answer. "Because they were people from other lands with too many stones in their fields for trees to grow in. They had to buy the trees if they needed them."

I felt sorry for those people. I had to do some more growing up before I could understand what my father was talking about. There were a lot more things which I did not understand, not then and not now. You never stop learning, I was told and I never did.

Since 1945 Memel is part of Lithuania and is called Klaipeda. I could not imagine that any more information would be found as to the origin of this distant relative of mine. In the war-torn region of the Baltic States it is not likely that even those files, to which we had access, still exist. I sometimes wondered though whether my arrival in Ireland, when it took place, was a venture into a new world or a return to my ancestral home. I gave these contemplations no serious thought because the *Shiels, Shiells or Sheils* to be found in the British Isles or Ireland spelt their names differently to my surname although the pronunciation was and is exactly the same. As time went on, I believe, I discovered more about my ancestors.

1.

When I was born in 1926, Germany was a poor country torn by strife without an effective government. Under those circumstances it was easy for Hitler to step into the breach. He promised to put an end to reparations, to create jobs and ultimately prosperity. He was not even German. All his wonderful ideas were conceived in nearby Austria and the Germans fell for them as long as they gave hope for the future.

I was too young to understand politics. On rare occasions I watched men in uniform marching down the street, pamphlets being handed out and I heard people greet each other with the words "*Heil Hitler*" instead of "Good day". My parents did not use the new greeting and I did not know what the words meant, but a child is impressionable and once I started school I got used to being part of a society no longer 'as old fashioned' as my parents.

At first we lived in the remote outskirts of Berlin on a loop road where the changes in our lives hardly affected us. We rented a small flat in one of six council houses. The nearest other dwelling was the coal-man's house, half a mile away. There was no public transport and there were very few bicycles. The loop road belonged to the children. I am sure the idea was to build more houses there, but they never materialised while we lived in the area.

It was but a stroke of luck - or misfortune - that my father had accepted a posting to Berlin, and I became a true Berliner. I arrogantly shared the pride of all people who called the river banks of the Spree and Havel their home. Songs galore encouraged the harmless patriotism in much the same way as a Cockney will always defend his beloved London.

We moved to a different flat several times, each time just that little bit closer to the local *Rathaus* (town hall), where my father was a junior civil servant. Without a car or public transport the daily walking distance became very important. Besides, there were schools and shops to be considered as well. I was about six when we moved to a beautiful flat nearly opposite a tram stop. My mother swore she would never leave this place. The blocks of flats were built in a rectangle with a family-friendly courtyard, about three acres in size. It was landscaped like a park with sand-pits for small children, little red-brick huts for dustbins and gymnastic equipment for older children. The rest was up to the children themselves and soon there appeared an extensive maze, a small football pitch and a stage setting behind the dustbin huts. Some areas were out of bounds to mothers, like the patch of grass inside an enclosure where budding script writers and actors rehearsed. The final width of the stage was still debated, when my sister was old enough to be the leading lady of every play. She turned out to be one of the actors who, in later life, performed on many a stage throughout Germany. Was it a question of the courtyard giving her the idea or had a dormant wish suddenly found expression?

Thanks to my father's labours as civil servant, we could now afford to live in those surroundings. He had taken two exams and on the strength of the results was promoted. We rented a two bedroom flat, had a large lounge for recreation, a fair sized kitchen/dining room and bathroom. Every seven years another girl was born, another sand-pit occupied, another bed put up in my room. We were now three girls and I often had to help out wheeling the pram with whoever was in it. More often than not I parked it in the courtyard while I read a book or played a game, having persuaded the baby to be nice and quiet. We children were devoted to each other although my persuasion did not always pay off.

The number 71 tram went by the estate on a single track every twenty minutes to link up with the *S-Bahn* (electric train) network. This single track was as long as the cemetery wall and the tram stopped but once, at the cemetery gates. A grocer had his shop below us, where you could buy the bare necessities. For more variety you had to go further afield.

Most important of all, the schools were, without exception, within easy walking distance from any of the flats. For a semi-rural situation there was quite a selection of schools: elementary, central, and both boys' and girls' grammar schools; a little further away a technical college and more elementary schools. The grammar school pupils paid a twenty mark per month fee; the central school pupils paid ten marks. If I remember rightly, my father earned between 150 and 160 marks a month. My twenty marks a month school fees were quite a chunk out of his pay packet. The deciding factor as to which school you could attend depended on your exam results. These exams were taken at the age of ten, and if a father could not afford to pay the fees of the proposed school, I believe the State paid for the education. The State also decided who could or could not finance their children's education. Records for such information were easily available, but it was a delicate subject which adults as well as children tried to avoid.

Three lakes, one large and two small, in mature parks were part of the suburb, and meandering sledge tracks had been laid which provided no end of fun during the winter months. There was a cinema nearby, an athletic sports ground, games pitches and riding stables. Alas, there was no television, no fast food, no refrigerator and no washing machine. Those were the conditions in which I grew up.

In the corner of our lounge stood my mother's piano which she seldom used. At some stage, aged seven or eight, I must have voiced the wish to have piano lessons. Also within walking distance lived a concert pianist, a lady whom my father often referred to as the 'fallen star'. She had indeed earned her living playing in halls throughout Berlin, but had finally decided to become a teacher, hopefully a good one. Heavily made up, over-booked and super-rich, she took me on, initially twice a week, for both theory and practical work. Hugs and kisses were lavished on me, until I appeared without having practised what I was told to do. Then the 'studio' would erupt. She threw my music at the door, told me to pick it up and then get out. I had been taught to pray at night. I must admit I often skipped that ritual, but during the first year of learning the rudiments of music and playing technique, I never ever forgot to say lengthy prayers when I walked through the park to my piano lessons. In later life my parents often wondered why I had never mentioned her temperament to them. I just did not. Perhaps I was ashamed of not having practised and of course, once rattled, I could not remember that Bach and Händel were born in the same year or what this or that Italian word meant. Now, with a lot of experience behind me, I can only say that she was not a good pedagogue. She failed most of her pupils by not passing on a love for music.

Thankfully she must have detected some talent in me for, after a while, things began to improve. I enjoyed what I played, because I could do it well and I realised that if my parents paid for the lessons, it was my duty to practise, but there were still lots of things I preferred to playing the piano. I liked the music well enough, but I hated performing at concerts every year. This was how the teacher advertised her teaching skills which just did not suit me, however much the papers praised my performance. My playing in public finally ceased, because either school or home commitments prevented me from preparing for the concerts. I understand that my teacher's fame finally rose to the level where her picture appeared on posters in underground stations, at least in East Berlin. In the end she became a dear friend to me, to the point of trusting me with her secret of hiding some Jewish friends from the authorities. I was still writing to her from Ireland in the 1960s, but the letters were so heavily censored that little of interest remained on the pages.

In 1936 the Olympic Games were staged in Berlin. I was very interested in listening to broadcasts about the Games. I would have liked to go to the Olympic Stadium and watch the track and field events with my own eyes, but my parents had other commitments. Naturally lots of foreigners had flooded into Berlin, and I made do with looking out for some of them. With my autograph book I combed the streets for unusual sightings, and I was not disappointed. Turning the corner, a Negro came towards me and smiled at me through pure white teeth. I had never seen a black man before and asked for his autograph. As luck would have it, he spoke some German and wanted to know, "Why?"

"I collect signatures of rarities," I replied with the wisdom of a ten-year-old. He burst out laughing and had the grace to sign my book.

Also, it must have been around that time, I remember a visit to relatives who lived in the centre of the city. My parents had promised the visit and since there was a girl of my age living next door, I quite looked forward to that trip. Their home was a cellar flat, where they had to descend a flight of steps to get to the front door. Those were the flats allocated to servants, who were butlers to high-ranking officers or government ministers. After brief greetings I excused myself and asked to be allowed to call on the girl next door. We hugged each other like long lost friends, sauntered down the *Wilhelm Straße*, had a look into this street and that and finally sat down on the bottom steps of the *Reichstag*. I wished I had brought my autograph book, but whether Hitler would come out or be as gracious as the Negro was doubtful. After a while a black-booted SS man told us to clear off. My friend was not surprised and pulled me to the pavement and round some iron railings or temporary fence where no-one could chase us away. We were minus a seat now, but we could see every bit as well as from the steps.

A black limousine pulled up opposite the steps. First the driver emerged who then opened the doors to his passengers and there they were: Hitler and the little fat man with what appeared to be a black flower pot on his head from which hung a tassel. "Don't you know who that other man is?" asked Ilse. It was obvious that I did not know. So she put me right. "That's *il Duce*, our Mussolini." Now I was really sorry I had not brought my autograph book. It must not have been a scheduled arrival, or else there would have been cheering crowds. "Shall *we* cheer?" asked Ilse.

"You can if you like." I paused. "I don't like the look of that SS man. He could kick me and then my bum will be as black as his boots. Next time we come visiting," I went on, "I'll bring my autograph book. Then we'll cheer. If I get a signature, I'll put up with a black bum." That was my suggestion then, but there never was a 'next time'. I never saw the two men together again. Hitler on his own, yes, I saw him a few more times, but not with the same enthusiasm as on the first occasion. I do not know why, perhaps because my autograph book had since landed in the dustbin.

During the summer holidays we always visited my grandparents in Treptow. Although I had become a true Berliner, 'wasch-echt' (dyed in the wool) they still call it, I always looked forward to going to Treptow. My grandparents had built a house there with three flats. They let two of them to pay for the mortgage and lived rent and rate free in the third flat.

Attached to the house was a garden, my grandfather's pride and joy. I shared his enthusiasm for gardening. As soon as we arrived I was out in the garden which, I am sure, had been manicured for my benefit. We always missed the strawberry harvest, but whoever had a garden would also have at least a hundred preserving jars. So there was always something left for us, be it strawberries, cherries, peaches or apricots. As for gooseberries and currants, gardening becomes fun when you can pick and eat while you work.

The downside to the property was obvious and serious. Each flat had only an outside toilet and a pump in the yard in place of a working tap in the kitchen. All provisions regarding water and sewage had been made in the would-be bathrooms and kitchens, but the council was slow in implementing promises of laying the pipes outside. We had to boil the washing in the cellar or outhouse, then pile it on to a cart and pull it for twenty minutes to the river for rinsing. Proper platforms had been built for that purpose all along the river bank, but the effort of getting it all done was enormous and so time-consuming. I always felt I must be careful and not dirty any clothes.

Without a doubt, Treptow's main attraction was its nearness to the Baltic Sea with its beaches - just ten kilometres away. Although other families had bicycles, we did not. So we walked with a sandwich and an apple. I still remember the beautiful smell of drying cut corn and the ever-present sunshine. The little seaside village we were heading for was called Deep, a familiar word to the reader, which shows how similar the north German dialect is to the English language. It simply meant what it said, which I discovered in later years, when I rowed from the river Rega out onto the Baltic. The river had dug itself a *deep* bed, way out past the edge of the surf and had left the whole estuary prone to fast currents and eddies. The Baltic Sea has no tides but can be very rough at short notice. Fishermen, who tied up their boats by the river bank, had a great respect for the estuary and the sea beyond. In the evenings they landed their catch of plaice and tied up right beside the promenade. They loaded the grills on the other side of the walkway with fish and sold smoked plaice wrapped in a newspaper there and then. When I first encountered fish and chip shops in England, I remembered Deep (now a part of Poland and renamed *Mrzezyno*).

Back home I had started grammar school. Children did not wear uniform; they were just spruced up for the great occasion. Having learned to write in the old German 'tombstone' script, I now had to learn to write in Latin script, because the first foreign language was on the time-table - English. I need not explain how difficult it is for a child to develop two different handwritings. We had the option to do that or switch entirely to the Latin script. To my parents it seemed sensible for me to do the latter since, in time, French and Latin would be added to the curriculum. I would get confused, permanently switching from one to the other. It was a fault of the system which demanded changes. In fact, elementary schools had already been given guidelines for teaching only the Latin script to all pupils.

The English teacher soon appeared on the scene and took our breath away. She was about thirty, had quite a sweet face with two very thin plaits curled round her ears and she wore a long black sack of a dress. She must have had several of those, because I never saw her in anything else. She was English herself with an excellent command of the German language, and she was the best teacher I have ever had. The other children were of the same opinion and the result was automatic respect. When she entered the classroom, we rose as one body and stood motionless until we were told to sit down.

At our first meeting she told us that her name was 'Understood', and that she wished to be addressed as 'Miss Understood'. How should we have known what they called people in that far away country? Later, doubts arose. My husband was convinced there was some trick or cover-up, or that I had got it all wrong. That made me furious, because I called her by that name for years. She had nothing to hide, but all my efforts in later years to find that name in a telephone directory failed; Underwood - yes, but not Understood.

Her teaching methods might be interesting to would-be language teachers, for she spent the first week or two on practising unfamiliar sounds, not used in the German language. The 'r', the 'th', and the 'w' are some examples. I still remember her words after seventy years: "When you leave this school, I want you to speak the King's English, so that people in England will suspect you to be a native and not some ignorant foreigner." That was all very well when you started from scratch, but we had an American girl in the class with that country's drawl in her speech. She was constantly in the limelight. "Look, dear," said the teacher, smiling at the American girl, "English was a pure language until your lot came along - no fault of yours, of course."

I am not debating here whether English is or is not a pure language. Which language is? To us, however, it was important to be as good as Miss Understood and to this day I often wonder why educated Germans on television, or living in this country for years, cannot shake off their German accent. They have never learned to do so; they cannot have done. I can still hear her. "Keep the sides of your tongue against your top teeth when you say 'r' and let the 'r' come forward in your mouth. Don't gurgle in the back of your throat. Now, try again and when you walk home after school, practise the three letters all the way home and all the way back to school tomorrow. That is your homework for today." We did better than that, we coughed and gurgled all through our lunch break as well.

As time went on, she would only speak English to us, constantly correcting our pronunciation. She so varied the lessons that they were a sheer delight, probably because she peppered all with a sense of humour. The achievements of her classes were far ahead of those of other schools.

We went to school six days a week and stayed until two in the afternoon, at that age perhaps only to one o'clock. For Saturday afternoons we often found extra school activities posted on the notice board - maybe a match, chess tuition or swimming lessons, or even a trip to a museum. Several subjects must have been important enough to warrant daily lessons. They included: German, English, Maths and P.E. The scientific subjects were taught three or four times a week. Religious Education, Art and Music came in last with one lesson a week, but of longer duration. The school activities soon fell into a predictable pattern. My interests were aroused in a different direction.

I came home one day and out of the blue announced that I had joined the Hitler Youth. My mother was clearly upset because, once in such an organisation, you could never leave. My father turned his back on me and walked out of the room. Only recently had he joined Hitler's party, because it was either that or losing his job. As a civil servant he was part of the government, but there were ways of keeping well clear of voluntary work for the party, and he was good at finding excuses when he was supposed to go to meetings. He came back into the room to talk to me on those lines.

I would have none of it. I had talked to the girls who had joined up and listened to their wonderful tales about camping and making lots of things out of silver paper and felt during the winter months. What I liked best of all were the reports about the singing lessons every Wednesday. So, without asking my parents, I had stopped at the youth leader's flat on my way home and signed on the dotted line. Fancy a girl of eleven signing on any dotted line, but that was how the authorities tracked down dubious parents. If you complained that your daughter did not know what she was doing, and could her signature be cancelled, you were a marked man. My parents were wise to those tactics and found more subtle ways of dealing with the problem and that was at a time when you could still attend any church service and had never heard of concentration camps. At that time the party seemed relatively harmless. A member might not have wanted to attend a meeting, but if he had left word that he or she could not come, and it did not happen too often, all was well. The youth movements offered so many incentives which were appealing to the young people that many children joined without their parents' consent. Highly qualified leaders and propaganda experts lectured in schools, and there was nothing a headmaster could do about it. How harsh the treatment of even dedicated Hitler supporters could sometimes have been is shown by the following account. In this case a father had initially received a letter of condolence, praising the sacrifice of a brave man, his son, who had died for his country. However, at a later date a friend of the deceased called on the bereaved father and put the facts right.

It happened during the war. A lad in our street was in his last year at the local grammar school and his marks were often less than average. Then an SS officer walked into the classroom and promised dispensation from all final exams - an automatic pass - if the pupil joined the SS there and then. Having joined the SS, this lad was trained and then sent to the eastern front where he was captured by the Russians. He escaped, but when he joined his unit again he was sent back to the enemy, this time with strict orders not to return. As an SS man, he was told, you do not become a prisoner of war in the first place. No more was heard of him and so ended a young life which may only have suffered a final 'fail' in the examination results. Maybe this kind of punishment rarely happened. I can only repeat what the father told me.

My time in the female branch of the Hitler-Youth, the B.D.M. (*Bund Deutscher Mädel*), was most enjoyable. We went camping in the summer and were promised art classes in the winter. Most of all I enjoyed the singing. The leader would sit there, with her instrument across her lap, teaching us new, rousing marching songs which I then harmonised. Other girls came over to me to learn the new part, until the sing-song was well balanced. Compared to the dull music lessons at school, it was a real tonic.

When I sang them to my mother, she asked me what I thought of the words.

"We march for freedom and for Hitler with the flag of youth,

For today we own Germany and tomorrow we own the whole world."

The words lose their impact on translation, but they serve their purpose. My mother had related that whole conversation to me in later years. On that day, she went on probing. "Who does the land belong to, which you are going to own tomorrow?"

"Nobody," I said. "We wouldn't take it away from anybody." Deep down I knew that every country was owned by its own people. I quietly left the room, not very proud of myself. Gradually a few more realisations about the Hitler cult nibbled away at the foundation of my belief. I stood shakily on a pedestal which had started to rock from side to side.

A few weeks after that talk with my mother the two Jewish girls in my class were missing. I knew the Jews were disliked and accused of, amongst other things, hating the Germans, but I had got on very well with one of them. She certainly did not hate anybody in my class. Now she was not there. According to the form teacher, both girls had moved to Bavaria. I did not believe that. My friend, I knew, had no relatives in Bavaria. Besides, she would have told me that she was leaving. Only yesterday we had walked home together through the park. Her father was a dentist and they owned a nice house not far from our flat. I was totally confused. The two girls had nothing in common. What had made them decide to leave at the same time, to a place they had never seen before?

I took my troubled mind to Miss Understood. She could not enlighten me without putting her job on the line. "Try your B.D.M. leader," she suggested. "She might know." I called on the leader on my way home. We always got on so well. I felt sure she would help me, if she knew. "Those two girls," she pondered, after I had told her why I had come, "weren't they Jews?" I nodded. "Well, that explains it." I did not understand. "Explains what?"

"How should I know who has taken them and where? Somebody has got sick of them and arranged for them to be taken away. They haven't told me where that was. Look, don't take it to heart and just try to grow up." She looked at her watch. "I must run. See you on Wednesday." She closed the door and left me standing there, until I turned and made my way home. My thoughts were in turmoil and somehow I resented Miss Understood knowing that I had joined the Hitler Youth.

I think it was during a medical examination at school that a doctor diagnosed in me a tendency towards rickets. We did not know what that meant. Did I have the disease or not? No-one seemed to know. I had had all the ailments I could think of. One more or less did no longer surprise me. In fact, nothing surprised me anymore. My mother and I were ordered to the health centre where I was told to attend gymnastic lessons on a daily basis and I was prescribed a vitamin-rich diet. My mother and I agreed of course, and she was handed a written note to sign. I was still allowed to go to school and do my homework, and I could work on my piano playing as well, but all other activities had to stop in favour of my strict gymnastic exercises.

The following Wednesday evening my mother accompanied me to the *B.D.M.* meeting. She produced the written note from the health centre and asked the leader if I may be excused from attending further Wednesday sessions. The leader looked at me with compassion and stepped back a pace. Her eyes scanned my face and limbs as though I was suffering from an infectious disease. She did not shake my hand. "Of course, I understand," she said without sincerity. "You must get better. I really do wish you well." My mother was already half way through the door with a smile on her face. She would get me better, now that that meeting was out of the way. For my part, I went to the gym regularly. I presume I am still a member of the *B.D.M.* because I was never discharged, but I never attended any more meetings. In time my health was fully restored and I excelled at many track and field events, at swimming and, above all, at competitive rowing. I raise my glass! "Here's to the *B.D.M.*!" For me it had been a scare which had never been allowed to take root. I must have been removed from the register as a kind of doomed creature or else the authorities had more important developments to worry about. They simply forgot all about my membership.

I made good progress with my piano playing. At twelve I played a selection of Chopin waltzes at a concert, at fourteen it was Beethoven sonatas. All this playing came to a temporary halt when my piano teacher injured herself on her yacht. A sailor had looked after it while it was moored on one of the big Berlin lakes and he had also taken her out in it at weekends, weather permitting. On that occasion the boom had crashed down onto her hand and all but severed the thumb from it. She was laid up for months and stopped teaching for the time being. Her hands were her bread and butter.

One day she took me aside. Would I go for lessons to someone else? It seemed a shame to break off my progress. I thought she was ill at ease to say all she had on her mind. The person she wanted to teach me was a Jewish lady. I said I would go anywhere she sent me and so I discovered her little secret. Next to her bungalow stood a three or four storey house with some accommodation at the back where she protected a number of Jews. I don't know how many or in what way she looked after them. I must have told her about my Jewish friend, and she naturally assumed that I was sympathetic to her cause. She was right on all counts, and the following week I was introduced to a middle aged lady with an expensive grand piano in her room. I had no need to probe into her circumstances. I went there to learn, I paid her the same fees as I had done before, and we got on extremely well. When my teacher was fit and well, I switched over again, and no outsider knew that I had ever gone to anyone else. The captives, I was later told, survived the war as well as my teacher who was extremely lucky to have done so. I learned no more about those captives when I made enquiries at a later stage. I believe they had eventually moved into a well-built outhouse attached to my teacher's bungalow, because the tall tenement buildings at the back had been pulled down.

When I was thirteen years old, war broke out. The reports about the reasons for such drastic moves were so obviously influenced by propaganda that one read every newspaper between the lines. Every foreigner was accused of having betrayed Germany. The Poles' ill-treatment of the German minority sounded unimaginably cruel. That could not possibly have been true, but the worst culprits were the Jews. I do not know where all the pictures supporting these accusations came from, or how they had been produced, but they were very convincing. My father, a veteran of the First World War, shook his head. My mother cried. I stood in the middle, an arm round each of them.

2.

When the war started my father put a map of Europe on the wall in the hall. There he recorded the swift advance of the German Forces, first of all through the disputed Polish Corridor, then through the whole of Poland and the Baltic States.

Hitler wisely stopped at the Soviet border and turned his attention to the West. The festering sore of the Corridor had been removed. He could afford to celebrate with his friend Mussolini. The few times I saw the news reels at the cinema, the German army drove through the countryside, someone else's countryside, and I remembered the *B.D.M.* songs which I had sung to my mother as well as the discussion that followed.

As yet the war did not affect us. My father stayed in the council offices, in reserved occupation. His office organised the distribution of ration cards and coupons for shoes and clothes. We had always lived quite frugally, so that even these new measures hardly affected us. We were neither on a starvation diet nor did we lack a wholesome pair of shoes.

Around that time my piano teacher discussed with me the possibility of relieving her of some of the less rewarding pupils. Was I interested? The arrangement was that these pupils would pay me half the fee my teacher charged. My sister, Erika (Eka for short), would be included. There were altogether six boys and girls, the majority only slightly younger than I was. I accepted the deal with great pleasure. My parents could now save the fees which Eka would have had to pay, and I could pay my school fees and for my own piano lessons. It was a huge financial help for the family and still left me with some pocket money. The price which I had to pay was also huge, for I had hardly any time to play or get out into the fresh air. I sat late in the evenings bent over my homework with the result that my school work began to suffer. I enjoyed my work though and never took the time to think about the pros and cons. I had no idea what might happen tomorrow, so why worry about today.

A great disappointment awaited me at school one day. Miss Understood was leaving. She had found a position as head of a language college in the west of the city. We were all sorry to see her go and eventually lost contact with her. I think she was happy in Germany and, although not a Nazi sympathiser, she put up with the regime. She was convinced that Hitler's reign could not last long and, if she held out that bit longer, she would experience better times. Perhaps people had made fun of her in England; in her choice of clothes and with her name, if indeed it was her name, she would surely have been ridiculed and yet she was such a champion for speaking the King's English.

During that time another event took place which altered my life considerably. There are few children who have not had pranks played upon them at some stage in their school life. I was no exception. I had received a new red leather pen case for my birthday and during break time at school one day the case vanished. My father had grown up in very poor circumstances and to suffer the loss of such an item seemed unthinkable to him.

When, after a week, the pen case had not been found, he made an appointment and stormed into the headmaster's office, demanding some action. Of course, no-one had owned up to hiding it and the headmaster washed his hands of all responsibility. My father responded within seconds. He would take his daughter out of that school which was not the only one in the land.

I was registered in another grammar school, the second of five, which involved getting up an hour earlier. I had to take a short tram ride, change twice on the *S-Bahn* network, pay for a fairly expensive season ticket and land in an inner city slum area. I had to do my homework on the train, half sleep-walking in and out of the carriages, text book still in my hand and I was secretly pleased when, a year later, the area was destroyed in a bombing raid.

If ever my father regretted a hasty decision, it was taking me out of the local school. He often said: "Why had I not shouted 'good riddance' when the case was lost?" Why indeed? Incidentally, a week after this - for me - 'tragic' event, the red case arrived in the post. It had been found on the top ledge of the black-board. Here we failed to learn another lesson. My father should have gone back to the school, put his pride in his pocket and asked if I could come back to my old school. I had been very happy there. Alas, he could not bring himself to do so. I still have the red pen case and sometimes look at it with mixed feelings. In a way I can also understand my father. It would not have hurt the headmaster to show a little more interest in the matter. The case could have been found a lot earlier.

Years later, in Braunschweig (Brunswick) around 1946, the three of us met again. My father and I took an old pair of shoes to the cobbler and there, hammering away on an old boot, sat my old headmaster. Both had outlived their usefulness. He had fled Berlin and the eastern sector before the Soviets arrived, found no work as a headmaster and had to retrain as a shoe repairer. When my father was quite sure who the cobbler was, he put out his hand. "Good day, Herr Doctor. We meet again." The headmaster looked up sheepishly and then entered into the spirit of reconciliation. Without retraining to do a job in demand, he would have had no money. He asked what I was doing and intended to do in the future. Was I still the owner of a piano, because I could play so well? His wife was dead and he lived in a bed-sitter. Judging by the look in his eyes, he did not mind whether he lived much longer either.

Continuing with my account of life in Berlin, the staff of my new school now welcomed me. Compared to my lessons with Miss Understood, the English classes were not really enjoyable, the teachers for German and P.E. made up for it. It was much the same story with anyone changing schools. You lost some and you gained some. In the upheaval I had not noticed that religious education had been scrapped altogether in all schools. At first some excuses had been found, but later no explanation was needed.

I threw my efforts whole-heartedly into P.E. and by the end of the year I was good in most aspects of sport. I attended the rowing academy once a week where we were taught to use the oars properly and how to roll in our seats. To help develop the skills, long, concrete 'boats' had been let into water basins and were fitted with all the latest equipment. They included hollowed out oar blades which created hardly any water resistance. Come the summer, we were out on the Wannsee, one of Berlin's bigger lakes, rowing 'fours' and 'eights' in competition against other schools. Sadly, that only happened once a week.

I remember going to the indoor athletic championships, having entered my name for the high jump. I was told Hitler took a keen interest in all those activities. He was not present on that day, but the Youth Minister was, judging by the fuss that was made. I never saw anyone I knew and I was not interested in who was present. There was just a sea of faces. At a signal I slipped on my black shorts and took my cardigan off, putting the shoes carefully beside it. I always competed barefoot now, inside and outside. I had no suitable footwear anymore; those shoes had been thrown away long ago and could not be replaced.

I surprised myself when I cleared the bar as the last competitor. I cannot remember what the actual height was, but that was not the point. In those days you only had one thin leather mat to land on, the other side of the bar. I was briefly junior high jump champion of the whole of Berlin. That mattered to me. Everybody looked stunned. I belonged to no club, had neither coach nor trainer and seemed to have descended from nowhere. Suddenly swarms of people wanted me to join their club. I did not know there were that many to choose from.

I was given a voucher on receipt of which, I was to be issued with a pair of spiked gym-shoes. When I finally obtained them, I found them to be of such excellent quality that they should have been kept in a glass case. The availability of any kind of shoes was virtually non-existent at that time. If you were desperate, because you needed a bigger size, you had to produce valuables in exchange. We simply repaired our shoes with strips of hardwood, glued and nailed under the sole. Unfortunately there ended my sporting glory. I had no time to devote to it, nor did I want to give up all other activities in my life.

I was asked what it felt like, being a champion. "Like a star that had dropped from above into the Wannsee, a star that never had a chance to shine." However, when I looked at my new spikes, I knew it had all been worth it.

The sledging experience was an event which was talked about long after it had taken place. On this particular day Eka pleaded to be taken out sledging. I needed a break anyway, so off we went. At the front door she jumped onto the sledge and let herself be pulled to the nearest park. The temperature was well below freezing and the ice of the lake so thick that it would hold any amount of kids and their sledges. Ours was a well-made, wooden one with extra supports and iron runners, on which I usually sat at the back steering, with Eka nestling between my legs. We would mount at the top of the track, cascade downwards slalom-fashion, round this tree and that object, shoot onto the lake, race across it and come to a halt on the opposite bank.

My attention must have been averted while I put on her gloves or tied her boot lace. Whichever it was, when I turned round, the sledge had gone. There were a lot of children around. We searched everywhere until we tearfully headed home. My father was cross. Wasn't I old enough to keep my eye on the sledge? He did not mean it angrily, but I felt hurt. There would be no new sledge that winter, maybe next year. The matter rumbled on for another week and then stopped, but I used every opportunity to look out for it. I would know that sledge in a hundred. Besides, it had my name heavily inked-in underneath one of the laths. I had no illusions. The thief would hardly return to the scene of the 'crime' with his newly acquired sledge, but some thieves are stupid enough to do just that.

This particular one had just arrived at the top of the slope and was ready to mount, when I intentionally stumbled and in falling against the sledge, turned it over to check my name and there it was. I righted the sledge and stood up, staring at a boy about my own age. I had never seen him before, and he must not have known that I was, in fact, the previous owner of the article in dispute. There were always too many people at the starting point. I felt my fist tighten inside my mitten and then I smashed it into his jaw with all the force I could muster. He staggered, not expecting the attack, lost his balance and slid down the icy slope on his backside. There was just time for me to shout: "That's for stealing my sledge, you miserable creature." More abuse would have been lost in the ever increasing distance between us and he must have made his way home without his ill-gotten gain. I was the happiest person on God's earth and hurried home, the sledge bobbing behind me on its string, like a dog who had found his mistress again. This had been a far better way of settling the argument than involving parents or police.

Needless to say, there was great jubilation within the family and for a special treat I took Eka out for a spin across the lake. She had missed the thing more than anyone. It was getting dark when we finally turned in.

Gradually the war began to bite. We could get no vegetables. The meat and fat rations were completely inadequate. Bread, also in short supply, had a peculiar look as though it had been made of saw dust. Coffee was ground of acorns, was bitter and sour and tasted like fermenting vegetables. I could not face drinking it and made do with boiled water with all meals. We could not buy milk until my youngest sister was born. She was christened Waltraut, but we all called her Trautchen.

During her pregnancy my mother had suffered from all sorts of ailments and after the birth she nearly died from septicæmia. Both breasts had rubber tubes running through them, continuously draining the pus. Antibiotics were not on the market, and so your constitution either successfully fought the condition or you died. My mother was treated at home, the doctor calling every day. My father had to stay at work and earn the money for our keep.

I was the obvious person to help out, at that time aged fourteen. I was taken out of school and my piano lessons were suspended, but I kept my pupils. We seemed to have got used to that extra income. I had to learn to cook gruel for my mother, feed and bath the baby and do all the other things which bringing up a baby entails. Very soon she was only happy in my arms, and I was the only one who could get her off to sleep. I tried to cook something for my father in the evening, but it was often over-cooked, under-cooked or burnt. He never complained.

I invented concoctions for Eka and myself. They kept us alive. We went out to the lane across the road, picking dock leaves and nettles which we chewed or boiled, and I bartered for the odd cabbage against anything I could find in the flat which might have been useful to the owner of a garden. All the hedges in the courtyard were of wild roses, and at harvest time you had to be out at the crack of dawn to pick hips. Otherwise some one else would have beaten you to it. My efforts would have been more successful, had I been able to go further afield, but I had to be about to look after my mother and the baby.

If that were not enough, air raids became more frequent. We could not move my mother into the cellar, so we all stayed in the flat. An anti-aircraft defence system had been built in one of the nearby parks. It was elaborate with guns and searchlights above ground and corridors, offices and sleeping quarters below. Special chambers held the arsenal to last a permanent war. While the system was functioning, it and a few others must have been dreaded by enemy aircraft. Once caught in the point of intersection of two searchlights, the pilot had hardly time to say his last prayer, or so we were told. It was no propaganda, for a little later I saw it happen.

In the meantime my mother's health improved. She eventually looked after the baby and did some cooking. That gave me the opportunity to travel to the countryside, call on some farmers and do some serious bartering. I now returned with a rucksack, bags and boxes full of unheard of luxuries like potatoes and eggs, flour and sugar. The farming communities had all they needed; the cities could not feed themselves. There were provisions and quotas to rectify that affair, but in the end the farmer just had to grow a bit more or feed a few more animals, without feeling the pinch. Some of the bombed out city dwellers, who had nothing and could buy nothing, showed open hatred against well fed country folk. The soil in Pommern and Ostpreußen (East Prussia) was excellent, and landowners seemed to have plenty of it. However, no-one would have wanted to swap places with them towards the end of the war when the Soviet soldiers rampaged through the land. They would pillage all in their path and kill whoever was in the way. Such was the hatred towards the Nazi regime and anything German, which had inflicted so much suffering onto the Russian people. There was no mercy now.

Finally I went back to school, and we did our bartering at weekends - the whole family setting off, pram and all. During the week, whoever was available would help organise the cellars a bit better. Every tenant had a few square yards of space down there, where he kept winter potatoes, coal and obsolete pieces of furniture which were too good to throw away. A rough timber partition divided individual 'glory-holes'. With frequent air raids becoming the norm, the partitions were ripped out and made into bunk-beds. Here and there a mattress was found until, in the end, every family had at least one place for someone to sleep. Soon an old table and a couple of chairs appeared and a second bunk was fitted on top of the first one. The residents of No. 20 embarked on open-plan living at night, sleeping, snoring and chatting in perfect harmony. Some residents started to move into the cellar before even the siren went. I could never understand that. Although, I must say, we had created a most comfortable place below, particularly after bits of carpets and screening curtains enhanced the shelter. Very often it was only a false alarm, an enemy aircraft passing over the outskirts of the city bound for other places. We would not know and the authorities took no chances.

At the end of the cellar was a back door and behind that a flight of steps which led up into the courtyard. We sometimes crept out to see for ourselves what was happening. The flak hammered away from the nearby park and it seemed like a dozen searchlights lit up the sky. "My God," said an old man, "There are thousands of them." It was a sobering thought which sent us scurrying back into the cellar, where someone else remarked, "Did you see that one come down? I reckon he was right over the cemetery when he caught fire. You wouldn't know who to feel sorry for - him up there or us down here." Not all were as magnanimous in their views, but I mention this one, because he actually said it.

We lived from day to day. Trautchen could barely walk when she joined the theatre group in the courtyard as some kind of angel. She was mostly very quiet, but could learn very fast. I had to learn the words of a little English poem, and by the time I had rehearsed it a few times, she knew it as well. She had not the slightest idea what it meant, but she was word perfect. She was always holding on to someone's skirt or burying her face in it and she was very thin, but weren't we all?

One day, as we had expected, my father's call-up papers arrived. He was then 43 years of age and was ordered to join the artillery on the western front. I knew few details about his posting, except that the cannons of his unit were huge. They sat at the German border and could not be moved, and there my father stayed until he was taken prisoner by the invading Canadian troops. *Feldpost*, special paper for use when writing to troops, could be obtained at the post office free of charge and so I took a pack home with me and wrote to him whenever I had a few minutes to spare. He greatly enjoyed the letters which were his tie to his family.

My mother had hardly recovered from her illness, when her father died in Treptow. I was taken out of school again to look after my sisters, while she went to Pommern to bury her father and comfort her mother. She would not be away for long, and we had food in the house to last that long. Children are very adaptable. When the siren went, Trautchen got up and brought me her coat, which I helped her put on. She put on her hat and picked up her little suitcase from under her bed. The case held all her valuables. It was perhaps six inches by ten, and in it she had a shoe-lace, a piece of string, a small rubber ball with a hole in it, a sheet of paper and a crayon. There was also a very small home-made doll which she called 'Miss Understood.' Trautchen had no other toys. When I see the toys which children have now, I cannot help thinking of her.

I did not leave the cellar during raids. I had promised my mother that I would not. Instead, I listened to the whining of dive bombers, bombs exploding and flak activities. Mercifully our housing complex was never hit. We lived fairly well at the very edge of the city with no factories within miles of us. My mother was terrified about leaving us, but she knew that I could cope, and neither of us could prevent an act of God.

When she returned I went back to school. My father's salary arrived at the end of every month punctually so we never had money worries, not real ones. On the strength of that, I gave up teaching the piano. It was all getting too much for me and school had to be my priority. Three months later my mother's mother died and I was taken out of school again. I had never been close to the old lady, not the way I was to my grandfather, but I felt sorry for my mother who struggled to cope. We walked her to the tram when she set off again. This time she had only to make funeral arrangements and then return to us. She did not have to comfort anyone left behind. Indeed, she was back within four days of leaving.

That first evening my mother and I considered our options. We could either stay put, or we could move up north into what had now become my mother's house. Some interested parties still had to be paid off, but that was easily manageable. As a family with small children, we were constantly urged to move out of the city for our own protection from air raids, but we had always refused. Now circumstances had altered because we had a second home in Treptow. We could grow all the vegetables we needed and more for bartering. There were no air raids and in walking distance was a boys' grammar school, which would surely accept me as a pupil. In hindsight I wonder what kept us from packing up straight away.

To the list in favour of going to Treptow I must also add that I had recently joined a class in the fourth grammar school, which I hated. The journey to and from school was even longer now, and the staff were so old, that our Latin master kept falling asleep in the middle of the lessons. On the other hand, I really liked my piano teacher and I loved my cousin, Irma, who was my own age and enlightened me about all the latest pop-songs and film stars. She was so lively and jolly that it was a tonic to be with her and we often visited each other. There was another cousin; older than I was and who was a really good friend to me. I would miss the two girls.

My mother had the final word. I am sure she made the right decision when she announced that we were leaving. She made arrangements for the continuation of the payment of rent to the council. They had a key to the flat to get access in case of emergencies, and my mother kept her own key. I gave in my notice at the school and said a tearful good-bye to the people I loved.

Although we had few clothes, a pile of belongings was gathered for which room had to be found in a case, bag or rucksack. Pots and pans and bedding were all in the new place. That left personal belongings, documents like birth certificates, exam results, school reports, photograph-albums, sheet music, to name but a few. When going on holiday, it had always been my job to carry my father's fishing rods. We decided to take them as well, as he would now come to Treptow when on leave. We all sat down and wrote a lengthy letter to him. Even Trautchen scribbled something on her sheet of paper and parted with it, since it was for her Daddy.

I had to write one last note to the organiser of an English language course which I had attended. I was so bored with the progress in English at my third grammar school that I applied for a place on that course. It was a refresher course for language teachers, journalists and, for all I knew, spies. I was the only teenager in that class, having passed an entrance examination. The young tutor always provided us with English newspapers, and then concentrated on current affairs. That was one other activity which I hated leaving behind. Although my duties at home precluded me from attending regularly, I looked forward to going when I could and I wrote to say I was sorry to leave.

Finally, we said good-bye to neighbours and made our way to the cemetery gates, waiting for the tram to take us to the main-line station. In years gone by, we had always travelled third class, where you sat with your back to the window on a long bench right round the compartment. In the middle of that square was a large space occupied by prams, sacks of potatoes or boxes with livestock. For the first time we now travelled in style - second class. We no longer had any need for the bulky luggage that required a lot of floor space. We treated ourselves to the express train, which could cover the journey in less than four hours without changing trains anywhere - quite a change from stopping at every village platform and taking over six hours to get to Treptow.

About thirty minutes before we arrived at our destination, we passed the gates to a concentration camp. The words *"Arbeit macht frei"* (work gives you freedom) made no sense at all. I think most adult Germans suspected that behind those gates lived the Jews who had once been their neighbours. I honestly do not know how they knew, because no-one, to my knowledge, had ever returned from such a place and told the truth about what went on behind those gates. No-one had ever been allowed to visit a resident of the camp or write to him or her. So where was the freedom, proclaimed outside the gate?

We were told and taught that the Jews had been our downfall in the past. They were to blame for everything and therefore had to be kept segregated in so-called ghettos. Towards that end, accommodation had been provided for Jews in special camps where they worked, using their skills until a more permanent settlement could be arranged for them. For the present, it was enough to prevent them from spoiling our chances of winning the war. Göbbels' propaganda always found the right words to satisfy his party members and his leader.

The fact that those camps were put up in very isolated areas, set people thinking. You did not have to be intelligent to do that, but while there were still Jews walking the streets wearing their yellow stars, people assumed that only a small minority had been sent away. We had no reason to complain about any of them. The Jews we had had dealings with were only kind and friendly people. There was our dentist, the surgeon who had operated on my mother, the lady who had given me piano lessons and the two school friends who had disappeared overnight and there were lots of others. Those people were an asset to the whole of society, not just to the residents of a camp. People who had watched deportations and street battles in Jewish quarters voiced their fears to friends who, in turn, had witnessed unpleasant scenes at police stations or at political gatherings. Gradually the horror stories reached the men and women throughout Germany and let there be no mistake, the German people knew very roughly what went on in the camps, but none of them could have imagined the extent of the brutality with which the Nazi crimes had been carried out.

Now, any survivors of the Hitler regime must carry the guilt for the atrocities which were committed in the name of the German people. Many Germans did not agree with this kind of justice because they said they were not involved, but they had tolerated that state of affairs with or without detailed knowledge, and history is now judging the collective guilt of the German people as harshly as the atrocities demand. Maybe, at this point, we should also remember that those atrocities were not only inflicted on the Jewish minority, German protestors without Jewish roots and members of student organisations suffered in the same way. They were all silenced - guilty or not guilty.

I wanted to demonstrate in this book how the young people of my age were won over to a regime which had evil intentions but had found a subtle way of persuasion. Only the total collapse of the regime and the Nazi element within the armed forces could now be the final solution for Germany. Years later, when I was shown a film about the Belsen concentration camp, I watched to the end and then broke down. In my opinion, the death penalty was inadequate for the perpetrators.

Have we learned from Hitler's mistakes? Is there no more genocide and torture in the world today? Certainly not on that scale, thank goodness. I sometimes wonder, though, how much and how long it would take to persuade a person, who enjoys inflicting pain, to join the staff of a would-be concentration camp. With the right incentives and the ultimate threats; with the right measure of hate and power; anything is possible. (So say I in hindsight).

On that particular day, when we were already nearing our destination, we fell silent for the rest of the journey, thinking our own thoughts. A brief shower of rain had made the countryside smell so good and fresh, as we discovered when we let down the window. When trying to identify the smell I have always claimed it was a mixture of vegetation and cow manure. Outside the station a little boy waited with a cart and looked at us hopefully. "Just what we need," called my mother and beckoned him to bring his vehicle alongside. The pieces of luggage were quickly loaded, and in less than ten minutes we opened the door to our new home which we knew so well. The 'driver' or 'puller' was given a generous tip and skipped off with his noisy cart in tow. My first inspection was the garden. Having only been used to a balcony, the area to be cultivated seemed to be enormous. I knew though that the garden would mean survival for us.

3.

The town of Treptow (now in Poland and called Trzebiatow) is an island town. It was built on the piece of land inside two arms of the river Rega. Some people named both arms the same, since it was the same river, and others called the narrower arm 'Mühlengraben' (since it served as a mill race). In the middle Ages it was, no doubt, an advantage to be surrounded by water and only to permit access via a bridge, which would have been closely guarded. A thick red-brick wall was the second line of defence. If enemy troops should have breached that, there was still one of the massive towers left. From this the inhabitants would pour boiling gruel onto the enemy when they were half way up the ladder to scale the gate.

In time, houses were built on the exposed side of the river, but not so many and ours was one of them. When we moved to Treptow there were some 10,000 people living in the town.

My new school was called Bugenhagen. The man by that name had spent much time in the town and had translated the Bible into Plattdeutsch ('Low' German). It was a dialect spoken throughout the region and thus he had provided the country folk with a readable Bible. Martin Luther was supposed to have been his best friend.

Another hero was celebrated - a soldier. He had owned a summer residence in the park at the edge of the town, which was now a kind of museum. His name was Field Marshal von Blücher. Amongst other exploits he had ordered the Prussian Army to mount their horses and, with him at the head of the column, they headed for Waterloo to assist the Duke of Wellington.

A third event made the town famous in 1944. Film crews and actors arrived, and scenes of a Napoleonic war were re-enacted.

The historic battle had taken place near Kolberg, some 20 miles away, but that town was now judged to be too big to represent the conditions of the previous century. We were delighted to have the filming moved to Treptow. The population of the town crammed into the market place, all dressed up in the fashions of by-gone days. They sang rousing songs and did really well. The senior pupils of our school all had to say a sentence or two at appropriate times, and the fun lasted for a week. My acting ability had been tried to the limit and had been found wanting. I understand the film had its première in Berlin to the accompaniment of Soviet artillery fire. It was also shown to U-boat crews in northern France, anything to teach the Germans more patriotism and put more pressure on them with yet more propaganda.

I can only say that living in the past suited Treptow. Coming from Berlin, it seemed strange to see wealthy landowners arrive in carriages for their shopping and to see people bow and curtsy when such a vehicle drew up outside a store. That was Treptow, one or two centuries behind the times.

Having been accepted in the school, I now had to find my way, both geographically and emotionally. It was a pleasant walk across the Blücher Bridge with the field marshal's name in broad letters let in to the concrete of the parapet. Immediately to my left I could then half slide down a grassy bank and land on a foot path known as the *Poets` Walk*. Situated between the town wall and the river was some kind of no-man's-land which finally ended in a side street, at the bottom of which stood our school. It took me about fifteen minutes to reach the building.

Facing the gable of the school, just the other side of the *Poets` Walk,* was the bank of the river and there, I noticed with joy, stood the school's boats' house. As I soon found out, it accommodated some six wooden skiffs of varying sizes. They were always maintained to perfection by a caretaker. What impressed me even more was the fact that the senior pupils had a key to the boats' house and could help themselves to any boats they wished. We often rowed a skiff a couple of miles down stream to a beauty-spot and sat there, doing our homework. Not quite so often we rowed the ten kilometres to the banks of the Rega at Deep, camped there and then headed on to the Baltic Sea. Once we had negotiated the mouth of the river, it was sheer bliss.

We had athletic facilities, swimming baths and a gym hall which left the subject of P.E. well provided for in such a small town and there the advantages ended. The school had taught Latin from first year and was only just starting to teach English. This meant that I had to take extra lessons in Latin, without a hope of catching up, and in English I was told to find myself an English book in the library and lose myself at the back of the class for the duration of the lesson. All other subjects, thank goodness, fell in line with what I had learned in Berlin and they were taught until we received our final certificate - the *Abitur*. All marking was done by the teacher who had taught us. Arguments in favour of that practice suggest that the teacher of the relevant subject, after all, knew us best, but this method does lend itself to favouritism.

I was one of four girls in a class of boys, and my appearance had caused quite a stir, not because I was bad in Latin or good in Music. I had gained notoriety before I ever set foot in the classroom. Whatever the pupils did not know about me, they knew that my uncle had a grocer's shop in the poorer quarter of the town, and that, on whichever day it was, he sold herrings from a stall in the market. The pupils from that school all had parents with professional backgrounds. I only remember one boy who did not. From the earliest times in that school I called the town 'Snobs' Island' with a capital 'S'.

As far as I remember, of all the teachers in the school, the history master was the only Nazi and he dominated the scene.

He always appeared in the uniform of the SA (*Sturm-Abteilung*), the military wing of the party and better known as the *Brown Shirts*. He had endless arguments with the headmaster and other teachers, but in the end they all backed down, for they knew their safety might depend on doing so. I was at that school for about eighteen months, and during the whole of that time we studied Hitler's book *Mein Kampf* with him.

A few months after I had left school, the Soviet army and some associated eastern troops conquered Treptow. They could not find the history master. He had changed his shirt by then and disappeared. So the headmaster was grabbed instead and publicly hanged. I am glad I was not there to see it. In any case, that did not happen for quite a while.

I had worked very hard at that school, because I thought I knew what was at stake. What exactly that was, I could not explain. It did not look as though I would get a brilliant leaving certificate and excellent reports and, in any case, what would I do if I did? Would a university take me? Would there still be one standing in the land? Hitler had promised a total war. I was beginning to see what that looked like.

With the summer holidays approaching and despite angry protests by the headmaster, the senior pupils were ordered to join working parties, building defences on the eastern front. A few of the younger teachers were to accompany us, not the history master, although he was the youngest. We waited together at the station on the given day, boarded the train and got off at a village called Pollnow. After walking for a mile or two, we arrived at a scene which I will never forget. We had underestimated what was meant by 'working parties'. Thousands and thousands of civilians, airmen, navy personnel, old and young were digging fortifications as far as the eye could see. As it turned out, it was a line of double trenches which stretched from the Baltic almost to Austria. First came a tank trench, three metres deep and four metres wide, followed by an ordinary infantry trench. There was no mechanical equipment. Each was given a spade or a shovel and told what to do with it. Men from the labour service had already cleared the trees and other obstacles and guards from the *Todt Organisation*, armed and fearful of their lives, supervised the project. It was summer, so most of us slept where we worked. The barns were crammed full of the elderly and sick, for whom there was no transport home. The procedure was to work in terrace fashion. One shovelled on to a higher platform, from where someone else picked up the sandy soil to throw further up still. At the top a squad of people had to dispose of the spoils.

Finally I saw the completed job, all expertly camouflaged with boards and spruce and birch branches. I called it a 'grizzly piece of supreme art'. Thousands, I feared, might die along those trenches. The redeeming feature - for the Russians - was that they had seen the trenches from the air and had figured out that if they drove a tank into the ditch or brought a bulldozer to fill in parts of it, they could cross with ease. How right they were. Later I was asked if anyone had attempted to kill the guards. I knew why they had not done so and could understand the reasons for it. For that you had to be part of those times in Germany. The guards could feel quite safe. The pilots no longer had fuel for their aircraft, nor did the navy for their U-boats. If this line of trenches had one billionth of a chance to stop the Soviet army in their advance, if only until some other weapon could be invented, then these men and women would work until they dropped. The guards could have thrown away their weapons, for the workers had better things to do than waste time on the guards.

Before we left after toiling for two months, I took one last look at that ant heap, and I felt very lonely, despite the crowds of people milling around me. All that effort, I knew, was for nothing. Our hands were full of corns and blisters, mine not as bad, because I had done a lot of gardening in the evenings, but I felt that my piano playing was doomed. Where would we go from here? Was there any place left in Germany, where one could hide? Hardly.

After our extended 'summer holidays' it was back to school. I quite liked the girl sitting beside me. She was the daughter of the local vet, and she had a brother a couple of years her senior, who had not passed his final exams at that school. I believe he eventually became a wealthy farmer in the West. His father probably saw to that. The three of us used to go for a walk sometimes or take one of the boats out, but I was never invited into their house, and they never came to us. I had no other friends. All too often expensive birthday parties were the talk of the day, but I was never invited. I remained the 'new girl' from Berlin, who had upset the balance of town etiquette.

Much later I asked my father how he felt about the attitude of the people of Treptow, since he was born in that town. To my surprise he thought there was nothing wrong with it. That's how it always had been. There just had to be those who hovered on the bottom rung of the ladder, and those who belonged to the elite. I totally disagreed with him. I believed that we all had a chance in life. My father had been very anxious that I should go to the grammar school in Treptow, that my generation should drop its obsession with what we saw as 'snobs', but he could not work out how. As it happened, it only took a couple of months before the attitude of the inhabitants of Treptow was eradicated once and for all. We lost the war. So where did our family fit in on the scale of 'worthiness' now? I was left in confusion.

Our final exams should have been in the spring of 1945. They were brought forward to the autumn of 1944. We were tested in every subject orally and in written work. By the time I received my report I was miles away. I had passed, but I was very disappointed with my marks in my three favourite subjects: English, Music and P.E. I kept telling myself that I was in Treptow in order to survive. Besides, as I grew older my ability in P.E. would diminish. Music I could write off anyway and as for English? What good would that be to me? I should stick to the ladder rung which had been reserved for me by my ancestors and yet, I was determined that I would not.

Before I left Treptow, and after my eighteenth birthday, I made arrangements to earn the prize of my sporting career, the National Sport Medal. I had to achieve certain results in, I believe, ten disciplines in athletics and swimming. For those aged eighteen the medal was cast in bronze. Medals in silver and gold were earned later in life although the requirements expected were all the same. The medals were usually worn below the waist on a suit jacket. Alas, I had no suit jacket. The authorities after the war stipulated that the swastika be removed from the medal, which is what I did. Later in life, the suit jacket was no problem either, but somehow the medal looked best in a shoe box of odds and ends. I did not want to be reminded of my time in Treptow.

School lay behind me. My next assignment was the Labour Service. In a way this Service was a good idea. All young people were required to work for six months either on farms or in factories. I had heard of many good reports by other girls who had just loved that time of camaraderie and freedom from parental supervision. They felt they were growing up and, what was so important, they all came from different backgrounds and different parts of Germany. We were still fighting a war on all fronts. Fronts, which kept creeping nearer and nearer towards one point in the middle, where all would end in a big bang. That was how some people put it.

Before leaving home and Treptow, I put the garden into shape and helped to preserve fruit and vegetables in jars. I half-heartedly performed that exercise, because deep down I had a premonition that those things no longer mattered. The Soviet army was now in Poland, in some places quite near the German border. East Prussia would fall first.

The stories we heard could not be imagined. Women drowned themselves with their children in rivers and lakes. Those who left in ships were torpedoed, and thousands perished. The Russian people now had the chance of revenge for what had apparently been perpetrated by the Germans. Here, it is not my place to go into details, suffice to say, life was worth very little in those days. I had not seen the cruelty with my own eyes, but I had seen some of the victims who had escaped the slaughter. Had the Germans been so cruel in the first place? I had not yet seen the film about the concentration camps. After I did see it I would have believed anything.

I had my little case packed. The train would take me to Stolp with a long walk of several miles to an isolated camp. The place had an aristocratic name, posh enough to frighten me - Hohenzollerndorf. As far as I was aware, it only consisted of a few farms and was a good cycle ride away from the Polish Corridor. I was ordered to report to the camp that evening. I said goodbye to my mother and my sisters in our home. We cried a lot and my mother did not want to let me go. It was one thing to join the Labour Service in peace-time, it was quite another to do so in times of war, in times of a war that was all but lost. We knew what would happen if I defied orders. The whole country was riddled with trigger-happy militia entrusted with restoring a discipline which had long since evaporated.

"You wrote in my book of sayings that one needs only to do so much to fulfil one's duty, and do so much more for love," I sobbed to my mother, "and now I'll have to let go of that love and only concentrate on duty."

My mother could hardly speak. "You are not abandoning all that love. I want you to promise me to always love us more than your duty."

I nodded, picked up my case and ran out of the door and all the way to the station.

4.

S chlawe would have been a nearer station to the camp, but the express train did not stop there on that day. Aware of that situation, some sort of military transport awaited us at Stolp station. Quite a few would-be *Arbeitsmaiden* (working girls) travelled on my train, and about fifty others were waiting at the station. However many there were, they constituted the camp. Without this spell of work they would not have found a permanent job or a place in higher education. Each German was supposed to know what hard work preceded the appearance of a slice of bread on his or her plate. As an alternative you could learn how the industrial cogs and wheels turned, which made ours the great nation it was, had been or would be. If your six months service happened to be in winter, you had to put up with ice and snow, particularly harsh in the east. In the summer you laboured in the heat of the day.

On that day we huddled together at Stolp station, waiting for the transport, and when it arrived a head-count followed, an athletic leap into the back of a truck and off we went. We soon turned onto the road to Schlawe, since the camp was situated half way between the two towns. I have never found the name of the village we were heading for on the map, but I know it was there. I also remember that after heavy snow-falls we always debated whether to pull the laden sledge of laundry to Stolp or to Schlawe. There was really no difference in the distance.

Since it was dark when we arrived, we only saw rough outlines of the camp. We were greeted by all three officers running the camp. They were all female and included the camp commandant with the rank of major, the head of administration who was a captain and the quartermaster who was probably a lieutenant. She was the only non-German, although she spoke the language well. I believe she came from the Ukraine. The whole camp was run on Nazi military lines with military precision, starting with the raising of the flag long before dawn, return from work after dark and party lectures on Sunday evenings. We all expected these conditions, because enough girls and boys had freely talked about their experiences after returning home. It was a case of putting up with what you did not like and enjoying what appealed to you. After all, the experience only lasted for six months.

On arrival we were led into the day-room for a hot drink, with which we ate and shared the sandwiches we had brought. We were really too tired on that day to find out more about each other. We simply noted in passing that all was clean and tidy and the camp would be a pleasant place to come 'home' to after work. There were three pre-fabricated huts and we sat in the dining room of the first one. This hut also housed the kitchen and lecture room. One of the other huts served as our dormitory while the third was accommodation for the officers. The three huts were built on three sides of a parade ground and on the fourth side stood the flagpole. Before leaving the dining room one of the girls wished everyone a good night. The commandant, a middle aged woman with her fair hair tied into a bun at the back of her head, raised her voice. "In here we use the German salute – *Heil Hitler*". I later found out that few girls had experienced such a Nazi zealot in the Labour Service. It was our misfortune to serve under her.

The following morning, after an early breakfast, we were kitted out; a khaki overcoat, serge suit, felt hat, white blouse, sturdy shoes and long over-shoes for heavy snow conditions. For our working clothes we were given a thick pullover, an overall, a woollen hat, and scarf and woollen gloves. The hat was a form of balaclava covering the head and face, except the eyes, and suitable for temperatures of minus twenty Celsius or lower. All clothes had been worn before, but had been laundered.

It was difficult for the quartermaster to satisfy everyone's needs. We haggled and argued over our clothing issue, but there was a lot to choose from, and in the end we were all satisfied. I only remember wearing the 'dress uniform' on the day we finally left the camp. What a waste of time and money to have issued it in the first place.

We were divided into groups and were given maps to find our places of work. We all had to walk for several kilometres and the same back each evening. My group was involved in threshing corn from the day after we arrived until the day before we left the camp.

The air in the barn was always full of chaff as the farmer and his wife kept us continuously busy by bringing heap after heap out of his vast store-rooms. We separated the corn and filled it into sacks with our only help, an ancient machine which we started by swinging on a handle and stopped by pressing a button. If we stopped for too long, the pile we were working on would grow so high that it interfered with the working of the machine. There was a brief break of half an hour at lunchtime, when the farmer's maid brought a tureen of soup for everyone. It varied from a watery drink to a thick stew and if we ever complained, the farmer would give us a hunk of dry bread as well. "Don't say I'm not looking after you," he might have added casually. We got on very well with him and deep down pitied him for having to work and live on this God-forsaken piece of land which he called his farm. He had never been on holiday, and only a couple of times in his life had he walked to the seaside, which was less than ten kilometres away. Tongue in cheek, someone once asked him what he would do, when the Russians arrived on his farm. "They'll take me to Siberia, where I hope to see my sons again," he said in broad *Plattdeutsch*, for he could not speak the educated German. His answer sounded so pathetic, so resigned to his fate and so humble, that we started to wipe our eyes. From that moment on he was our friend, and at Christmas we packed a parcel for him and his wife with some of our treasured possessions. When he received it, as we found out later, it was his turn to cry.

That Christmas we also devised a method of each one of us packing up a little surprise for someone else. We did not know for whom. All names were thrown into a hat, and every girl picked one out, and that was the recipient of her gift. There had been a brief debate as to whether the officers' names should be included. In the end we agreed to show ourselves magnanimous.

As luck would have it, I received a gift from the quartermaster. There was a postcard-size picture of her (which I still have), a few bits of toffee which she had made with some left over margarine and a small piece of embroidery from her home country. I was very touched and genuinely thanked her. I cannot remember who received my gift, but my newly acquired connection with the quartermaster had pleasant repercussions.

At the end of the dining room stood a piano on which I often played tunes from memory, since no-one else could play. It had not been tuned for years and it was of unknown origin, but I soon discovered that playing it gave the girls and staff pleasure. One day the quartermaster took me aside. She had to go on foot to Schlawe. The staff had collected a little money to buy me some music. What should it be? I was delighted, and accepted gratefully. I prepared a list, bearing in mind the trend of the times and I included some classical favourites. I had not included Nazi marching songs although there would have been dozens to choose from. Finally I wondered what response my list would draw from the commandant. There were no objections and whatever could be bought from my list, the quartermaster brought back to the camp. I thanked each member of the staff politely. I knew now that my playing was appreciated and it gave me pleasure to relax most evenings, sitting at the piano.

The food seemed in very short supply and was unimaginative. Often we only received a dry piece of bread, but we all knew that there were many people who had less to eat and we rarely complained.

At weekends the commandant would hold regular lectures on the aims of the Nazi party, the new weapons that were already being tested and on the biographies of our leaders. We had heard those talks so many times before that we wondered who would still be interested. How come the Soviet army was now on our doorstep when everything was going according to plan? We listened with indifference but appreciated a relaxing sit down after a hard week's work. The back row of chairs was always in great demand because you could dose off there an odd time.

The commandant was a well educated person, and in later years I pondered over her feelings in those last weeks in the camp. She must have known, or at least contemplated the possibility, that she would be captured by the Soviets and she would hardly have had time to justify her position in the *Third Reich*, before being dealt with and at best being executed. In her daily routine she never showed any signs of frustration, fear or change of attitude. She was, I would think, true to her oath to the *Führer* to her last breath.

One evening she sent word to me that I was to report to her at ten o'clock the following morning. To make that possible, I was exonerated from joining my working party on that day. It was an unusual request and I could not help wondering what was in store for me.

I reported to her in her office as requested and waited until she had settled in her armchair. I was not offered a seat. She came straight to the point. "I have been asked to send one of the girls to a training college for potential officers in the Labour Service. The girl has to be educated to *Abitur* (A-level) standard, with excellent P.E. marks. She has to be or has to have been a member of the Hitler Youth and show leadership qualities. You are the only girl to come into question, the only girl who holds the *Abitur* certificate." She never took her eyes off me and, if looks could kill, I would be dead and no longer able to tell the tale.

At first I thought it was a joke. How could anyone expect to find volunteers for a Nazi affiliated organisation like the Labour Service at that time? It was just like signing your own death sentence. Since there was no trace of a smile on her face, I suddenly realised that she was quite serious. She wanted an answer there and then. I had to think quickly and be as precise with my reply as she had been with her statement because it was not a question or an invitation. I had to be convincing to be believed. She was still all-powerful within the camp.

Outwardly calm, I formulated my speech, although inside I was boiling over with revulsion for anything remotely associated with the current regime of our country. I began, "I must be grateful for the trust you put in me, but I had other plans when leaving the Labour Service. I wanted to study medicine." I don't know what gave me that idea. I thought it was a good one at that time. "My second point: It may be the norm to join and stay in the Hitler Youth until you join the party, but I was forced to leave the movement at the age of eleven."

"On what grounds?" She snapped.

"On health grounds," I replied. She seemed satisfied and I continued, "I don't know whether you managed to get hold of my last school report. If you did, you will find that I had very poor marks in P.E." Much as I had been annoyed with my P.E. teacher in Treptow and his biased marking, now I could have hugged him for giving me yet another reason why I should not become a leader in the Labour Service.

She was quick to respond. "I understand you have been junior high jump champion in Berlin." She smiled at revealing her trump card. Who told her that, I wondered?

"That was a long time ago," I said feebly. I was beaten and I knew it. Maybe a little sense of humour would brighten up the morning. "Now, if you had said the Labour Service was looking for a piano player - - ." She had no sense of humour.

"I think your high spirits want cooling off a bit. Go back to your dormitory; get changed into your sports' gear, singlet and shorts, and report back to me. Dismissed." I had an idea of what was coming. When I returned, she sent me out to stand in the snow, not only in singlet and shorts but also bare-foot. I watched the snow melt under my feet, but as they got colder ice began to stick to them. I cannot remember what the temperature outside was, nor do I recall how long I stood there or jogged there on the spot. It certainly was not for hours, and I obviously survived, but that was not the point. She had overstepped the mark. After a while she came to see me with a scarf round her head and dressed in an overcoat and gloves. On finding me shivering, she sent me to the dormitory to warm up.

I rubbed my feet, I bathed them in cool and then in warm water. I jumped up and down to restore my circulation. I fetched several hot drinks from the kitchen and finally crept into my bed. I was still freezing when some of the girls returned from work. They were livid when they heard what had happened. I was now in pain as the circulation returned. The girls did all they could to help. At one point they were asked to fetch their soup. One of the girls picked up my soup bowl and walked off. She had it filled for me and told the kitchen staff that the rest of the girls were not interested in their soup. So ended my Labour Service nightmare. The subject was never mentioned again, at least not in that camp.

After the war my father tried to trace the commandant, but she had made sure no-one would find her, or she had become a casualty of the war. I made my father give up the search for her. There were far more serious cases to follow up. I had survived – although he maintained I might not have done. I was not able to go to work the day after the episode, but that was all. The commandant had done herself no good. From then on she was despised and ignored by the girls, while in other camps a friendly relationship existed between staff and recruits. She must have felt very lonely.

The official payment for a day's labour was 25 pfennigs (a few pence), to be collected once a week on a Friday. It was mostly spent on postage stamps. In songs and jokes much fun was directed at this puny reward, which added so much clerical work for hardly any return.

Our stay at Hohenzollerndorf came to an abrupt end, when the exploding artillery shells made us cover our ears. The Soviet troops were still a good distance away, but their gun fire reminded us of their approaching presence. At short notice the commandant decided to wind up our stay at the camp. She gave orders to inform the farmers that no more working parties would be sent out. I do not know how the farmers were informed for they had no telephone and the postal service had ceased, but in those days every person had his or her own worries and solutions to problems.

We were to be ready within one hour to walk through the freshly fallen snow to Stolp station. Schlawe station was out of action. No trains stopped there any more. The walk would certainly be entirely through forest.

The quartermaster threw open the doors of the store and invited us to take with us whatever we could carry. Unheard of luxuries suddenly saw the light of day; butter, dried fruit, sugar, tinned milk, chocolate and all manner of tins filled with meat and fish. The holding back of all those items was perfectly justified, for the quartermaster had to stock up until at least the end of March. It may not have been possible to reach us during severe winter spells, but if we were to abandon the camp, we might as well take what we could. Those who were wiser considered what other things would have to be taken as well, for example a warm blanket rolled up on top of the rucksack, a change of clothes or a spare pair of shoes. The greedy filled their rucksacks with so many tins that they could hardly carry them. With food having been in such short supply for so long, we were conditioned to look after our stomachs first. After the first couple of miles, piles of food were thrown away because they could no longer be carried. Now there was a shortage of some warm clothes and at the brief stops some of the blankets and coats had to be shared, which meant that two girls huddled together inside one coat or under one blanket.

There was no turning back now and we did not blame each other or lose our tempers. "Together we stand or together we fall," shouted one of the girls. The commandant knew when the train would arrive. She kept looking at her watch. There were still five kilometres to go, but instead of at least keeping up the pace, the column of girls moved slower and slower, but in the end we arrived. There may have been less than a hundred people waiting on the platform. Most inhabitants had already left, but those who stood there were desperately worried that the train would take no more passengers and, worse still, not even stop.

These were all people who had left their homes for good. It was now a question of survival, because without a chance to make it to a place further west, these people believed that they were doomed. They may or may not have been right, but those areas close to the front line usually bear the brunt of indiscriminate violence and slaughter.

It now depended on how packed the train would be on arrival, as to how many would get inside the coaches or cattle trucks. One thing was certain; whoever could not get in would cling to the outside. Falling off somewhere was still better than being left on the platform.

We were all lucky, for when the train arrived, it could still accommodate passengers because it was very long, so long that I wondered whether one antiquated engine could pull that load at all. The train had started its journey just a few miles east of us and if it had managed to get to us, we stood a chance of getting away. That was another way of looking at our predicament.

To our horror we saw some *Wehrmacht* soldiers help two women out of the train. A grave was being dug with bare hands in a pile of snow, and two bundles were laid in it and covered over. Two babies had frozen to death and had found their final resting place at the edge of Stolp station. Whoever had seen the incident started to cry. We stood for a moment and then boarded the train.

Inside, the seats were automatically reserved for expectant mothers, old people and wounded soldiers. There were not enough seats to go round. Everyone else squashed into gangways and any empty spaces. Many children found a place to lie in the luggage racks. When no-one was left outside, the station master pushed his wife in and found a space for himself. He blew the whistle through the window, and the long snaking train started to edge forward. The train stopped at no other station for the next few hours, because there was just no more room left inside. If the engine had to stop, then it was in some woods or open fields. Maybe a dozen more people could have boarded, but people would have fought each other to the death, if someone had jumped the queue. It was the last train leaving that area, the last train heading west.

I saw no other graves being dug in the snow, although the engine driver stopped every four hours or so, to let people relieve themselves. Before he left, he always made sure that everyone was aboard. Nevertheless, people only squatted down right beside the train, so that if it started moving, they would have ample time to jump up and get back inside. Those who could not do so just stayed in the train. Perhaps they had brought some napkins. Such details were so insignificant at the time; I am surprised I still remember them.

Although we were heading west, progress was so slow that a journey, which might have taken six hours in a slow train, now took three days. Food ran out, but bundles of snow were reached in and distributed in place of water. I stood in a gangway next to a soldier. His age was hard to determine, anything between twenty and fifty. Caked with filth, a stick tied to his leg and a blood soaked bandage on one side of his face, he told me he was a law student from a place which later became East Germany. We talked on and off but only briefly. In the end I asked something which had preoccupied me for a long time. "Are German soldiers really responsible for all those atrocities they are accused of?"

"In so far as we have started the war, I suppose yes," he replied. "Russia never signed up to the Geneva Convention. The people were used to being cruel to each other. Given half a chance, they would be cruel towards us. We tried to have as little contact with the civilian population as possible. We tried to obey orders, and those orders did not include cruelty. There are always bad apples in every basket, but if you are looking for culprits, then try the SS. They were trained by beasts and a lot of them became beasts. Those are my views. I am sure everyone has different views and who is to say, which version is the right one."

"Thank you," I said, "for giving me your version. I know now that I'll have to work out my version." After that I never asked any more questions of that kind, not then and not later. We don't know half of what has happened in certain corners of the world, what a respected individual was and is capable of doing, be he a nation's leader or a casual worker. Human beings need to be held accountable. That is why a democratic government is so important.

After standing for three days in the gangway of the train, I suddenly passed out. No food, no seat, no opportunity to move my legs, no hot drinks - no wonder. In the meantime we had reached civilisation in the south east of Germany, and when the train stopped again, I was helped off and taken to a nearby Labour Service camp. I don't know who took me there for by now I had lost consciousness. I had still not left the war zone completely because the camp had already been evacuated, but there were a lot of people still milling about in streets and on roads, as I found out later.

A surgeon with the Labour Service was still clearing his desk. He lived in a nearby town and had no intention of moving away from there. Why should he? He had done no harm and he was tired of life anyway. He answered the knock at the door and received me on a makeshift stretcher, as though that was all part of his daily routine. After I had been carried into the surgery, the person or persons who had brought me left again. It must have been a very large camp, because we never had a surgery at Hohenzollerndorf.

I started to move before I opened my eyes. It was difficult to move, as though I had been strapped to a frame. Presently I came to. The surgeon tried to explain what had happened and then pointed to my legs, which lay on the mattress like two shapeless and useless tree trunks. He had had to cut off my boots. Both legs were full of fluid. He refrained from drawing some of that out, as he thought I would only produce more. He wanted my body to extract the fluid when it was good and ready. I had little medical knowledge and could not judge whether he was right, or whether he wanted to get out of doing a job properly. On the face of it, he seemed a very dedicated surgeon. I gave him the benefit of the doubt and did exactly as he said.

I was confined to bed for about a week. After that time I could already see signs of improvement. I started to go to the toilet on crutches, and eventually I tried on a spare pair of shoes, which I had brought in my rucksack. The rucksack, I was pleased to note, had come with me to this place, and gradually I was able to wash myself and some of my clothes. My uniform was all I had in the form of an outer garment. It looked pretty filthy by now.

I had two visitors every day. The surgeon came in the morning and an elderly lady brought me a hot meal in a can at lunch time and some bread and cheese or sausage wrapped in paper for all other meals. No doubt, the surgeon had organised this service.

One day, when she stayed a bit longer, I asked her if she knew a place, where I could get my uniform cleaned. She knew I had no money. It was, therefore, a delicate question. Apparently that was all looked after as well. The surgeon had told her that I was due some back pay which would cover all I needed in that camp. It might almost have been a kind of belated holiday there, had it not been for the explosions of Soviet shells in the distance. The enemy had again caught up with me, or nearly. In the meantime I had practised getting into my shoes, first without tying the laces. I walked on crutches through all the corridors for my allotted time of exercises until one day I was allowed to go out into the fresh air.

I was staying in a truly beautiful place, set in mature woodland, the *Thüringer Forest*. I had, of course, seen it through the windows, but that was nothing compared to being out in it. I walked along the little tracks with the beautiful smell of pines, which I had always loved. From then on, I only went indoors for my visitors and for my night's sleep.

Sometimes it was eerie on my own at night. Then, one day, I had company - a different enemy, an enemy I had met before in Berlin. Wave after wave of bombers brushed the treetops. There were no search lights and flak, no spectacle to watch, just a deafening drone. Since the electricity had been disconnected in the camp, the pilots saw no lights below them and at that low altitude must have felt quite safe. I figured that we were the distance of the height of a tree apart from each other, and at that I was as safe as they were. If I was going to make a habit of staying out after dark, I had better organise some ear plugs. I did just that during the following day. As anticipated, the bombers were back again, but when it started raining, I went inside.

I had no idea where they were heading, maybe Dresden or Leipzig. If not the pilots, some of the crew would have been my age. Gosh, I burst out laughing; some of them might even have known Miss Understood.

The noise in the sky kept me awake and it was late when I finally dropped off to sleep. There seemed to be more aircraft than ever coming or going. Why did there always have to be wars?

One morning the surgeon appeared bright and early. He carried a briefcase and invited me to take a seat opposite him at his desk. The purpose of this early visit soon became apparent. He felt the time had come for me to leave the camp. My legs were making good progress, although I was still using crutches. For that reason, it would be better for me to depart at my leisure than to be hounded out by the enemy. Where did I want to go? I explained that I had only one relative in the west of Germany, in Lüneburg, and that I was hoping that my mother would make it to that town as well. Ultimately, if my father was still alive, he would expect us to go there and would want to join us there.

He filled in a form and then handed me a document, confirming my discharge from the Labour Service on health grounds. To my surprise it said that I was suffering from rheumatism of the left shoulder. "Don't take any notice of the wording," he smiled. "According to the book of words, rheumatism is accepted as one of the reasons for a discharge, your legs wouldn't be." In addition, he produced a travel warrant to Lüneburg. He put out his hand and wished me God's speed and a lot of luck. There would be transport to take me to the station, say at nine o'clock in the morning. The train to the nearest city would leave a couple of hours later. "Would that be all right?" I nodded and tried to express my sincere thanks for all he had done for me.

When the lady brought my dinner, she also provided me with a substantial packet of sandwiches for the journey and a bottle of 'lemon juice'; there would hardly have been real juice in it, but I looked forward to drinking it. "Oh, and was the uniform cleaned all right?" I said it was and she confirmed that she had received any payment necessary. She chatted to me while I ate, and I discovered that she was a distant relative of the surgeon and had found employment in his house. It was probably only temporarily. Some families were inclined to provide support to one another in troubled times. Others, as we will presently see, could not get far enough away from each other. These conditions must be well known in any part of the world.

Next day I rose early, already feeling excited about what awaited me. I would meet different people. I would see my relatives. I might even link up with my mother and sisters. I shut my eyes and ears to war scenes and war noise. For now I was free and would take whatever happened in my stride.

On that day everything worked according to plan. A small Volkswagen military vehicle *Kübelwagen* arrived at the door. The driver helped me into it and put my rucksack beside me. I took in one last, long, deep breath in the hope of taking some of the pine scent with me. Then we drove to the station. I never saw the surgeon again.

At the station the driver left me and returned to wherever he had come from and I studied the scene around me. There were very few civilians. The military made up for that and, of those, nearly all were wounded from the eastern front. By that time the eastern and western fronts had moved closer together again, so that soldiers from the western front could be seen returning to their homes in this area, in what later became East Germany. The part of Germany further east was now out of bounds and where I had last lived, no-one would want to go back to anyway. I found it surprising, therefore, that the soldiers with homes here did not anticipate that their part of the country would be overrun as well. It was only a question of time, but to help loved ones in their hour of need was an overriding desire of most of these soldiers. The consequences of those actions never seemed to occur to them or matter. To die with your loved ones was, for most of them, preferable to perishing on your own.

It was easy to distinguish between travellers from the east and those from the west. Those from the eastern front no longer wore shoes. These luxuries had long since been worn out and had not been replaced. In place of shoes the soldiers wore strips of sack cloth or bits of uniform wrapped round their feet and they wore bandages somewhere, which were not only blood-soaked but also filthy. I felt conspicuous with my wholesome crutches. Many soldiers had to rely on forked branches to help carry their weight.

I made my way towards a few civilians and, after the train had arrived, I climbed in and looked for a seat. It was one of those coaches with a long corridor on one side and small compartments on the other. Presently I found a seat beside a young woman, a girl aged about ten and an elderly woman. The rest of the bench was occupied by wounded soldiers as was the bench opposite. In such confined space the air became stale very quickly. With so many unwashed bodies and infected wounds, the stench was certainly very unpleasant, but we had to put up with it because the soldiers were not in that condition from choice. We simply had to open the window an odd time and let in some fresh air.

It was only a question of time before the little girl asked, "Can we go somewhere else, Mummy? These soldiers stink like cow shit." A child does not understand perhaps, although that kind of language is not used in respectable homes. The mother's reply, "You are right, pet, we aren't a civilised country anymore," was an insult to any wounded soldier. In cases like that I was always quick to interfere and join in the battle. I wanted to punch the woman, but by now I had learned to fight my battles with words.

"You are quite right," I said. "With people like you about, we'll never be a civilised country again. Why don't you get out? That's what your daughter wants." I held the door open for her and waited until she had left. Two other soldiers took the empty seats and peace was restored. My companions were embarrassed and apologised. I told them not to be so silly and, in any case, I had had enough of it and wanted to go to sleep.

I changed trains twice. Each time the train was less crowded, but the proportion of civilian passengers to military stayed about the same. Passengers without shoes still dominated the scene.

On the last part of the journey I shared a compartment with just one other passenger: a pilot from Austria who had flown Junker aircraft. We had a stimulating conversation about Germany's literary greats and some of the German composers. It was refreshing to talk about some of the better achievements in German history, rather than engaging in endless war talk. His aircraft, he told me, was not usable for lack of fuel. I was not quite sure what he was doing on that train which was heading for Hamburg, another city in ruins. At one point I had unpacked my sandwiches and had offered him one. He did not seem to have brought anything to eat. The sight of food made his eyes light up, and he thanked me profusely.

The time passed very quickly. Suddenly, quite out of the blue, he said, "Will you marry me?"

I burst out laughing. "Is that because of the sandwich?"

"Of course not."

"The answer is no," I said, "and that's final."

There had to be an explanation for his proposal; he knew it and I knew it. From then on he did most of the talking while I tried to understand. I could not believe that there still existed such devotion to Hitler in his branch of the services. How could that be at such a late stage in the war, in a lost war? He had it all worked out. He would journey through the country, looking out for a girl of his choice. He would get married and travel with her to Austria. He would have at least seven children and hopefully boys, who would all serve the *Third Reich*, even after Hitler had gone.

I held my breath. Was he still sane? "I'll tell you one thing," I said after a while, "you'll not find a wife in Germany who will bear you seven Junker pilots for the next war. Catch yourself on and catch a train back to Austria and see if you can find a girl there."

The trouble was that I could not offend him. Weeks later he turned up in Lüneburg. He called on me at my place of work, to see if I had had a change of heart. I burst out, "Who the hell told you where to find me?" Someone in the job centre of the council had done so, and I was furious. "Get lost," I shouted, and walked away. He tried to make contact once more, I ignored him and he then gave up. I had met many people of differing view, I had come across extremes in the most unlikely quarters, but he stands out most vividly amongst them.

❧

5.

At the time I first arrived in Lüneburg about 60 000 people lived in the town. It had a very picturesque town centre, almost medieval. Main roads in and out of the town went north, south, east and west with churches, convents, schools and hospitals all built in a red-brick Gothic style. Heading further out of town, you came across the private houses with lush gardens front and back. Although there were quite a few small factories operating throughout the town, they were not vital to the war effort. Whether for that or for any other reason, the town had suffered no bomb damage, as far as I could see. This made Lüneburg a most desirable place to be in. It was also in the west of Germany, by just a few kilometres as it turned out later.

I found my way to my uncle's flat, quite near the town centre, and to where he worked in the main post office in a reserved occupation. The house accommodating the flats was three stories high, and the flats, although only rented, were in great demand.

I took a deep breath before I rang the bell. My aunt opened the door. Neither of us recognised the other, because we had not seen each other for over ten years. I explained who I was, that I had recited a little poem at their wedding and I asked if I could stay there for a couple of nights, until I had found work. She looked at my crutches but, faced with such a spontaneous request, she was not sure what to do. Reluctantly she opened the door a little further and asked me in, to sit on a chair in the kitchen. She was a timid soul and obviously had to ask her husband first and he was at work.

Once inside the flat, I asked the burning question; had my mother and my sisters called on her? They had not, but suddenly the magnitude of an avalanche of relatives descending on her sunk in. Here I must mention that families, who had a spare bedroom, were obliged by law to take in a refugee family from the east or a bombed out family from the west. Was it not preferable to take in relatives rather than strangers? She could not deal with that problem on her own. She excused herself, put on her hat and coat and hurried to the post office to consult my uncle. He took time off to deal with the situation and arrived back with her in the flat. So far, there had been no greeting exchanged between us. Perhaps it was just as well that my mother had not come to this place. I had developed a thick skin in dealing with questions of survival, but my mother would have burst into tears, if her brother had treated her with so much indifference. He seemed to find lots of excuses. They had intended to put their son into the spare bedroom. There was no furniture in it. The one wall was slightly damp and the room could not be heated.

I listened to all this without comment. He may have formed the impression that I might go to the authorities and put in a complaint and, in any case, my mother had not arrived yet. She might never get that far and would it not be more sensible to put up with one lodger, than to have to take in a whole strange family? Somehow they remembered that they had an old mattress in the cellar, and there was a basket with spare bed linen down there as well. "See, what you can do," he kissed his wife. "I'll have to hurry back to the office."

"Can I make myself a hot drink?" I asked. I had not had one all day.

"I should have offered you one," she said touching her forehead, as though she was incapable of thinking about bed and drink at the same time. By the evening I had a comfortable bedroom with a made-up mattress on the floor, the rucksack beside me and the crutches leaning in a corner. I practised walking about the room without crutches. I had to learn fast, and I was surprised how well I got on.

By eight o'clock the following morning I had called at the labour exchange and was offered a job in a toy factory. 'Toy factory' is perhaps an exaggeration. It was a noisy shed where ten people worked. I made one *Hampelmann* (Jumping Jack) after the other, first cutting out the plywood shapes on the fretsaw, then sandpapering them and finally painting each finished toy. It was not as monotonous as it sounds, because for some 'Jacks' I would choose red for a jacket and blue for the hat, or green for the trousers and pink for the boots, but I could not picture myself doing that for the rest of my life. However, if and when I wanted to leave, I only had to give one day's notice. That suited me. At the end of the first day at work I asked if I might have a day's pay in advance and not wait until the end of the week. The foreman counted my finished Jumping Jacks and gave me a few German marks, for which I had to sign several pieces of paper and for which I could buy a loaf of bread and a few other bits of food on my newly acquired ration cards.

I went 'home' in the evening, delighted with my progress, but this delight was miniscule in comparison to finding my mother and sisters sitting on my single mattress in my uncle's spare room. Our rejoicing at coming together again was ecstatic. Sitting there side by side, we shared the food I had brought and listened to our different experiences of the intervening months.

We decided to go for a walk, find a quiet place somewhere to discuss our future, if only in the short term. Eventually, I listened to what my mother had to say about her brother. It came as no surprise to me. I tried to impress on her, that I needed a better paid job. They were crying out for nurses, so much so, that the training had been reduced to six weeks. If my mother could accept these living conditions for that time, I would have enough money to rent a properly furnished room somewhere. With my present wages, it was either a furnished room or food on the table - but not both. We debated our options. Could we find a baby-sitter for Trautchen so that my mother might go to work as well? In the end my mother thought her brother would get used to the idea of having relatives in the flat for a limited time. She would stick it out. I suggested we might think things over for a week and let me earn a few more marks. This might enable us to put a deposit on a room. We would then know where to go when I returned from the course. It seemed strange to engage in all this talk about money when there was so little to be bought with it.

To earn my living as a nurse had never occurred to me. In those days it was hardly better paid than a 'Jumping Jack' creator, but there was a difference and there were prospects of advancement and better food. In the end I could always leave and go in for further education, proper qualifications or a different job altogether. I made up my mind to hand in my notice.

We were still at war. Montgomery, it was said, was now biding his time not very far west of Lüneburg. There were still skirmishes, but a point had been reached, where the German soldier was much happier becoming a British prisoner of war than a Russian one. There were no other options open to him. Montgomery had slowed down his advance, perhaps until all his allies had reached their agreed geographical positions. Fierce fighting was still going on in the east, but the Soviet army made steady progress. The end of the war was certainly in sight. However, judging by the determination of the German front-line troops in the east, it could be weeks before Stalin had won all his battles. His list of casualties was certainly enormous, but it would appear that quite a few Soviet victims had been offered as 'cannon fodder', if you can believe that. Some Russian soldiers did not even have a rifle, we were told by soldiers returning from the front line. There have been exaggerations and rumours probably on both sides and maybe Stalin's men did run out of rifles or ammunition at some time. The fact was that the Soviet troops were fighting heroic battles just east of Berlin and the Germans fought back with the tenacity of dying men.

Our private family life must be seen against the backdrop of those external events. A brief discussion took place between my mother and her relatives. They were told that I would be going on a course in Lübeck. On my return I would live in the nurses' quarters, and at that time the rest of the family would look out for different accommodation. Until then my mother promised that she and her two younger daughters would cause as little inconvenience as possible. They would all sleep on the mattress already provided. It was a frosty family arrangement.

My uncle must have found my mother's plan acceptable and welcomed her and her children into his home. There was obviously a limit to her stay and that must have appealed to him. Some second-hand furniture could be bought and there were a few spring cabbages in the garden which could be spared and so on. In that atmosphere I said good-bye to my mother and sisters and, perhaps rather less sincerely, to my relatives. The four of us went to the station together. I hugged them all, boarded the train and sobbed all the way to the next stop. It was a moment in my life when I felt I had not properly grown up yet. Although I would soon be nineteen, I was still a child at heart.

The journey was short and uneventful. I had intentionally not taken my crutches, because I seemed to manage very well without them now. I would make sure, if possible, not to stand or walk for too long. On a nurses' course they would understand my caution. Besides, my mobility was improving by the day.

The first day on the course was spent sorting out formalities. I was given what seemed like a luxurious bed in a bright room for six students. I had a wonderful hot stew and I wrote and posted the first of many letters from there to my mother. None of those letters ever reached her.

In the days to come I learned how to put on bandages and splints, give injections, resuscitate casualties as well as the routine monitoring tasks of taking temperatures, blood pressures and peering into patients' eyes and ears. I do recall that obesity and age were no problem at that time. The elderly were part of a family and the shortage of food prevented people from getting over-weight. There were many lectures crammed into a day and I soon found out why.

Nurses were so urgently needed, that we would only stay on that course for three weeks and then, if possible, be sent to a hospital of our choice. Looking back now to my time of nursing, I can honestly say, of all the things which I learned there, putting on a bandage was all I had to know when I started work in a military hospital. All other nursing skills were not required of me. What was required was common sense and not to refuse any task, however menial and however far removed from the responsibility of a nurse.

I counted the days until I would be reunited with my family. I worked out where exactly I would look for a room. I even contemplated renting a flat, a very small one. There was as yet no news of my father. If he did come back, there would have to be a bed for him. I worked out how far my earnings would stretch and I dwelt on other irrelevant speculations. Then came the day when once again I stood on the platform waiting for a train, in my hand a piece of paper now authorising me to work in a military hospital as *Red Cross Helper*. I would collect my uniform in Lüneburg, to which I would pin a brooch proclaiming my newly acquired status and I would fling that Labour Service uniform into the first dustbin I came to. This time I thought that I knew it all.

I arrived at my uncle's flat with a spring in my step. My aunt opened the door and asked me in. When I sat on the familiar kitchen chair, she said, "Your mother and the girls have gone." Before that remark had time to sink in, I blurted out, "Why?" She busied herself with some cups and saucers, before turning to me again. "How should I know? They were here one day and gone the next. There was some talk of her travelling to Lübeck to pick you up. Where she had planned to go with the three of you, I have no idea."

"Did you have a row?" I wanted to know.

"If we did, then it was for a stupid, unimportant reason. Your mother had become very touchy. She cried a lot and then she must have thought of how to sort things out and just left. She never even said 'good-bye.' She certainly was no problem to us. We even put a wardrobe into her room."

"What did she want a wardrobe for?" I burst out. "She had no clothes."

"Well, I suppose to make her feel more at home. I even proposed all of us sitting at the kitchen table for our dinner."

"Did you cook for everybody?" I enquired. I had to get to the bottom of this. Here was a family with a well established garden and the opportunity to barter for fish and meat, for butter and eggs. I had lived there, I had seen it all.

"Now, that would have been difficult," she replied at last. "You see, she and the girls ate very little, whatever she could get on her ration book, which was not very much."

"And I suppose Trautchen wanted some of your food," I said with tears in my eyes.

"Well, your uncle likes to eat well, and we didn't have any to spare, not really, and your little sister was so fond of the plums which I'd preserved, but your uncle was fond of them too. Last autumn's harvest wasn't all that good. So, it was all rather difficult, but we managed."

I had heard enough. I enquired if they were owed any money, or whether my mother had left anything behind which they wanted out of the way. "No", said my aunt, and before taking my leave I suggested that they should get rid of the wardrobe, because they would not want a reminder of their lodgers and we would not be coming back. I picked up the little bundle, which I had brought, and my crutches and left. I walked aimlessly through the town, found a bench in a bus shelter and once more sat down and shed a few tears. I now had a good idea why my mother had left the town, but I still did not know where she had wanted to go with all three of us. That night I stayed in the bus shelter.

In the morning my face was a mess. I did not want to present myself at the hospital in that state. I went to a public convenience, had a wash and then headed to my new place of work. When asked in Lübeck, I had requested a return to Lüneburg, but the choice of hospital within that town was not mine to make any more. I do not recall how many hospitals there were. Every surgeon seemed to have his own hospital. Every spare hall seemed to have been provided with an operating table and some more or less competent surgeon put behind it. The town was swamped with wounded soldiers. They arrived from all corners of the compass, from all fronts with all manner of old or new injuries. I now looked for the piece of paper in my pocket with the address of my new place of work and when I had reached the hospital, I called on the matron at her private residence and reported for duty.

Originally a nursing sister in various theatres of war, she was now in her forties and seemed to spend more time keeping her staff happy, than finding specks of dust in the wards. She explained to me what kind of service was expected of me, and that that would have little in common with conventional nursing practice. Hopefully things would improve, but at present there was utter chaos. She urged me to be patient.

We had a meal together and then I received my new uniform. In future I would wear a white head dress with a large red cross stitched onto it, a grey and white striped dress and a white apron. There were also some stockings, underwear and a good quality pair of walking shoes. Lastly, I was given a warm, belted overcoat for the winter. Since we were approaching summer, I put the coat and stockings aside for cooler days. With the exception of coat and shoes, all items were duplicated because they had to be washed regularly.

I got on very well with all the staff and the experience helped me to mature, to grow beyond the impetuous girl which I knew I sometimes could be. I stopped feeling sorry for myself. Instead, I stood up for myself. I found the right answers for bullies and I gave orders, when I should only have been obeying them. If only my private life had been more settled, I could have been very happy there.

The following day I started work in the hospital. It was a converted grammar school, Gothic in style, similar to the nurses' quarters and there the similarities ended. Approaching the entrance, I saw a long queue of soldiers lying or standing round the building. They were all waiting to be attended to, at least to be called inside. I headed straight for the cellar, my place of work. Here, in double and triple bunks lay those wounded, who could not be moved from a ward every time the air raid siren went. The precaution, to put so many of the wounded into the basement, was understandable. Every night we expected air raids or heavy artillery fire, but neither ever materialised. At a guess there were three to four hundred men there. It was a vast basement space, in a way ideal for the purpose, but it had only two very small windows, as I recall, and lacked fresh air. It was, therefore, only temporarily used as a ward. In the middle of that 'intensive care' unit stood the operating table, a qualified nurse one side, the surgeon the other. Everyone here was anxiously waiting for the war to end.

The surgeon had run out of all but some sutures and cotton wool. There were no more anaesthetics, no more bandages. I was told that the surgeon worked day and night and when he could no longer stand on his feet, the nurse took over, performing minor surgery. I had no idea what happened when she needed a rest.

During the first couple of days I emptied urine bottles and wheeled the dead to the mortuary. As time went on, a soldier might ask me to pray with him. He might, when I passed, show me a photo of his family. He might offer me his Knight's Cross for the support I tried to give. He might even pay me a compliment when he was close to death.

On one occasion, when I was returning from the mortuary, two walking patients stopped me and asked if I would remove the SS emblem which had been tattooed on their arm. All SS men could be identified in this way. I told them that I was not qualified to do any kind of surgery. "If you belong to the SS fighting force you will have lost a battle, but you have nothing to fear. If you have committed crimes you will now have to be accountable for your actions. Anyway, I haven't time to chat about 'cosmetic' surgery." I left them standing there.

Shortly after that incident, several British officers walked into the basement. I believe they had an interpreter with them. All life came to a halt. The surgeon was briefly consulted, before the inspection team left. They had seen enough. The interpretation of that visit was swift and accurate. The town had surrendered to the British. There would now be no more obstructions for them, before linking up with the Soviet troops. Peace was imminent. All the wounded could be moved to the wards now. All the would-be patients lying outside could be brought in, but no new casualties would be delivered or queue up outside, maybe a trickle who had unsuccessfully tried to treat themselves, but that was all.

That and many other considerations crossed the minds of staff and patients alike. For us the war was over. The signing of the peace treaty, which Montgomery chaired on Lüneburg Heath, was just a formality for us. There were some Germans who were not even aware of it happening. Those millions of us, who celebrated the end of the war, were obsessed with the slogan of the day: "No more wars, ever."

Around that time a military van stopped outside the entrance to the hospital and about a dozen walking patients were collected for interrogation, included was the surgeon. He and a few others returned the following day. The rest of them were detained. I remembered the two SS men who had wanted me to remove their tattoos and I wondered if they had been collected. Apparently the British wasted no time in their search for SS criminals.

Little changed as regarded our workload, but we now received ample medical supplies, which made our work much easier and much more rewarding. Unfortunately there never seemed to be an end to the day's work. Without the tranquillity around the mature trees of the nurses' quarters, we might have gone mad. Evenings were the time to have a leisurely meal and stock up with sanity. Rarely did we venture outside those precincts. When we did, the only change to the town's image was a considerable British military presence.

Around that time we also had our first case of diphtheria. After preliminary tests, patients and staff were inoculated against the disease. It was then that I was found to be a carrier of the disease. Although I was perfectly healthy, I could infect anyone who came into contact with me. I had to stop work. I had to be isolated. I had to receive treatment and undergo constant monitoring.

The matron immediately volunteered to have my bed moved into her private residence. There I had over two weeks of glorious holidays and the only person I came into contact with was the matron. She brought my meals, collected my laundry and provided me with stimulating conversation in the evenings. I had never had it so good. She was a wonderful person and had her own story to tell. I was left spellbound by her courage and experiences of nursing in a field hospital during the campaign in Greece.

Spring had arrived in all its colours and with all its sounds. War or no war, occupation or no occupation, the seasons arrive every year. When my period of isolation ended, I was allowed to return to the nurses' quarters and was ready to start work. I was given responsibility for a ward on the first floor of the building. On my way upstairs a nurse caught up with me. "At the moment there are forty patients in or beside that ward of yours, thirty inside and ten outside, all amputees."

"Forty?" I cried and stopped in my tracks.

"Don't worry," she went on, "we're trying to move half of them to a room one story higher. We're completely over-stretched at the moment, emptying the cellar and bringing in all that lot from outside. Ever since your patients were moved up here, they haven't had their dressings changed and giving out food has been a bit hit and miss." I despaired. I pushed the door of the ward open but had to duck and withdraw as a barrage of some filthy dressings flew towards me. It was how the soldiers' expressed their anger and frustration.

I waited until all was quiet and then stepped into this large room, where the beds had all been pushed in, most of them double bunks. I figured I would hardly be able to move between them. I addressed this hostile crowd. "Now the firing has stopped," and there were, after all, only a limited number of missiles that could have been thrown at me, "I want three men with sound legs to come and pick up this mess here." Silence. "Three volunteers or I'll pick them out." I did not wait for long. "You, you and you."

"I've only got one arm," was the first complaint.

"That'll do," I said. "You only need one arm to do your picking. We'll find a couple more with one arm. They can hold the bag open for you."

I had asserted myself and was beginning to gain their respect, because deep down they knew that the more time they wasted, the fewer men would have their wounds seen to by the evening. Some more volunteers appeared on the scene of their own free will and all was quiet. Just one young fellow piped up: "Nurse, are you always that cross." There must have been ever such a brief smirk on my face.

"Only sometimes when you behave like children." A working party was formed to fetch water for drinking and washing. Other patients were sent to get the trolley filled with bandages and ointments, with sterilising powder and water purifiers. Some soldiers offered to empty urine bottles, because they could see that I would not be able manage it all without help. The battle could only be won if every walking patient contributed to the running of the show. They had to stop feeling sorry for themselves, and I knew I had to get hold of some crutches somewhere. There were none in the hospital.

At half past eleven I went to fetch the watery stew, and at twelve o'clock sharp my 'one-armed bandits' ladled the food into dishes and distributed them until the last man had been served. I rewarded my helpers with a cigarette each, which I had hoarded for some weeks and, while they had their meal, I walked across to the nurses' quarter to have mine. I felt I had the situation under control. What I did not expect was the number of volunteers on the following day. There was even a young man with no legs who thought he could do something in bed, if there was another issue of cigarettes. I told them I had no more. Besides, they had done so well without them that it would be a pity to start smoking again.

Their wounds gave me cause for concern. They seemed to be healing well, but they were all infested with maggots feeding on the pus. No matter how often I scraped them off and how often I dressed the wounds, they were always back again. I think it took me a whole week to get rid of the last of them. Sadly, no doctor appeared in the ward for a long time, but thank goodness, none of the patients in my care deteriorated. I probably went the wrong way about dealing with the maggots. My short period of training did not teach me how to deal with that kind of infestation.

Around that time half my patients were moved upstairs to a separate room. We now had room to move, enjoy more fresh air and get the place cleaned up. I even shared that chore with the patients, and I attribute their steady progress to allowing them to become more involved in their care. They had a purpose in life and were not labelled as useless.

My evenings were spent trying to find potatoes and crutches. An odd combination, but I felt that more food and more mobility would further speed up their progress. It would also make life more pleasant for the patients. I simply went to farms and negotiated for a sack of potatoes by pleading with the farmer's wife. She had probably also lost a loved one in the war. The next stage was to persuade the farmer to deliver the potatoes to the hospital with his cart. I went begging for fruit and vegetables for my patents and I need not enlarge on the enthusiasm when one day I wheeled in a trolley with fried potatoes and two eggs each.

Similarly, I would go to other hospitals and rehabilitation centres where maybe someone had finished with his crutches. I brought my own crutches. In that way I was able to collect all I needed although at first I sometimes had to make do with walking sticks. More importantly, I allocated the crutches in relays - two hours this one - two hours that one. It was the perfect solution, because in the end supplies came through again.

Occasionally a patient was ready to go home, if he had one. Quite a few left, others did not know where to go. For some their home was in what was now Soviet territory. Those soldiers lived in constant hope that their relatives would make it to the west, but at that time there was no postal service, so how would they find out? Letters were simply delivered to certain institutions by people who had walked anything up to a couple of hundred miles. Anyone on the move would collect letters and deliver them to a hospital or government office in a town he had wanted to go to or pass through. Across Germany relatively few people could contact one another, and many of them, like myself, had no idea where their relatives were. My mother would have had a very good idea where I was, but was she still alive? Were my sisters all right?

It was a sunny day when I arrived at work one morning, and walking up the stairs I met a soldier on his way down. There was nothing strange in that encounter, except that this one was my father. We hugged each other and cried a bit and then sat down on the stairs to ask each other a hundred questions which could not wait. One of my patients passed us and wondered what on earth had happened. I turned to him. "Tell the others to go and fetch their breakfast and keep a slice of bread for my Dad." He looked at me in amazement and simply replied, "If that's your Dad, we'll keep him two slices!"

6.

It was hardly surprising that on being released from a prisoner of war camp, my father had made for Lüneburg. His reasoning was that, if we had escaped from the east, Lüneburg would be the town we would have tried to reach. On arrival at the station, he had made straight for my uncle's flat. There he had learned where I worked and that the location of the rest of the family was unknown.

Now, at least father and daughter were together. After he had his breakfast at the hospital, I sent him to the *Rathaus* to get his ration cards and to look at all the notice boards where accommodation was advertised. We had to find a room for him. As mentioned before, all permanent residents of the town had to take in single people, families or returning soldiers who had no home to go to. The authorities decided how many people had to be given refuge in any given household.

Hopefully this accommodation would be in the same street as my hospital. I might have wanted to stay with him if he was ill, for he was incredibly thin. We might even be able to trace my mother one day. Then she would also have a roof over her head. At least there was one bread-winner now, until my father would find work. My pay was very poor, but it was enough to feed him and pay the rent for a furnished room. Until there was a new currency we could buy our rations but little else for money. Never had there been such a wide gap between the 'haves' and the 'have nots'.

We met that evening again. He had written down the one and only address of a room on offer in the desired locality. We went to look at the house. It was large, had three stories and was owned by a professional man and his family. We soon found out more details. They had been wealthy before the war, and they were still wealthy. Their bank account may have started to dwindle at one point, but by investing in more property in good time, they had hardly suffered any inconvenience or loss. There were three drawing rooms downstairs, opulently furnished, five bedrooms on the first floor and there was a second floor which was being refurbished at that time.

None of that should have been of interest to us. The room we were offered was high up in the attic. We were led up a fire escape to the second floor, through a door into a hallway, from there through another door into the loft and then over half a dozen ceiling joists to 'our' private door. Inside was a spacious room. The large window had a view of the street below and there were three beds with mattresses, a table, a small iron stove, a hot-plate and a cold water tap with a sink beneath it. To get to the toilet, we had to retrace our steps across the joists and enter the loft hall. Inside the toilet cubicle there was no wash-hand basin, no bath and no shower. We asked for time to think things over and left.

What we were shown elsewhere bordered on the ridiculous or pathetic. All rooms on offer were within someone's flat without any privacy whatsoever. We renewed our call at the first address, this time with certain demands, without which we said we would not be interested. We wanted a hot plate with two burners, a few strips of plywood across the joists where we had to walk, a light in that area of the loft and a shelf or small table in the toilet for a bowl of water.

The landlady knew that I might also be moving in and that the rest of the family might join us as well. All told, we must have made a good impression, because she found our demands reasonable and promised to have all done within a few days. Meanwhile my father could move in against a month's rent. She would even find a blanket and a sheet for him. I had no further complaints and the month's rent may have meant nothing to her at the moment, but it would be very acceptable if or when the new German currency would be introduced. That time had to come. As for the missing bath or shower, with so much space in the loft we would organise, beg or borrow a tub of some sort, heat water on the iron stove, pour it into the tub and revel in a few inches of warm water. There was no way I could have pressed her for more concessions, and the privacy of the place meant a lot to my father. However, as time went by she did have a cold-water-only wash-hand basin plumbed in the toilet and she provided a tin bath in the loft with a cold water connection. All we had to do was heat some water in a couple of large saucepans to warm up the cold water in the tub.

To find work for my father was a far more formidable task. There were no jobs on offer as a council clerk. No one was interested in retraining him at his age and in his condition. He was not a very versatile person anyway. Hard as he tried, he could not find work. He went to the doctor to see if he had a medical problem. The doctor found him too emaciated to do any work. He wrote him a line to that effect and for the next two weeks my father received social benefits.

Quite a few British units had taken up residence in the vicinity of where I worked. It occurred to me that there might be an opportunity there for him to find work - any work - part-time if necessary. We were not really interested in the money. He would be pleased to work for a midday meal, gain some strength and put on some weight. He spoke no English, and so it was up to me to act as go-between.

I hardly knew where to start. There were at least twenty addresses to choose from and I had no idea what the soldiers were doing there. One evening I called at the first house I came to. A sergeant opened the door. He was about thirty five, tall and fair. I politely asked in English if they had any unskilled work for a German civilian. "I suppose you want to know if we can be doing with a dog's-body. Come in, Nurse, I'll make some enquiries." He took me into a front room and disappeared. When he came back, he asked me a few more questions. I told him that I did not know what a 'dog's-body' was, and that it was my father on whose behalf I was enquiring. The sergeant laughed, explained what a dog's-body was and said they would take my father on. I was delighted. Pay was irrelevant, but would he get a midday meal? He would and he would be paid. I could not wait to tell my father and hurried off to his new abode. He was pleased as well but a little apprehensive about not being able to speak English. I put his mind at rest, because I had seen other German staff there as well and they would tell him what to do. My father settled down so well in his new job, that he kept it until we finally left Lüneburg.

I had to catch up with my own work now and only saw him twice a week perhaps. Patients were continuously reshuffled as more and more of them were fit to leave, but occasionally a new patient arrived. One such soldier had lung surgery. When he first appeared in my ward, he had a huge lump beside him under the bed-clothes. "What are you hiding there," I burst out.

He sheepishly pulled the sheets aside and said, "A violin, Nurse." The whole ward exploded into laughter, and straight away they had a nick-name ready for him. I was the only serious person there. "And you mean to say," I went on, "that you carried that violin with you from one posting to another and from being wounded to recovering here in one of my beds?" He nodded. "It's a good one, Nurse." I was speechless.

"Are you going to give us a tune one day?" I asked.

"I will have to practice first."

"Go on then. What are you waiting for?"

"Oh Nurse," came the complaints from all around him. "Do we have to listen to that?"

"You do," I said, "I've listened to enough of your stories and problems. Now it's his turn, just for half an hour, half an hour every day. You can take a walk in the corridor if you're too ignorant to appreciate music. You have crutches now if you need them. There is nothing to worry about."

The violin and its player gave no end of pleasure to all of us. He may not have had a polished technique any more, but he put so much feeling into his music that one could almost hear the violin cry at times. The crowning of his little practice sessions was the day when I found a piano in the basement. He came down and I accompanied him. For spectators there was standing room only, but the 'hall' was always packed. Alas, he also left us one day, and the bed remained empty.

At times I wondered now when I would be made redundant. The time would come. The building had to become a school again. It had served its purpose. I had no idea what I would do next. We did not have the means for me to go to university, and there was not a subject which provided sufficient interest for me. What I had excelled at had been neglected to such a degree, that I would hardly have passed an entrance examination in any subject. At one time I would have had a brilliant future in something; now I was barely average in everything.

A few weeks passed, and again a soldier was looking for me in the hospital. This time, when he had established my identity, he handed me a postcard written by my mother. She had written six such cards and given them to six different soldiers, who were heading for the West, in the hope that one of them would find me. I hope I had thanked the soldier adequately, because news from my mother was more important to me than anything else. I immediately began reading what it said on the card and by the time I looked up, the soldier had gone.

My mother was back in her beloved flat in Berlin. She and the girls had survived the fighting in the city. Now she lived with two other families in our flat and earned the daily bread ration by shovelling coal in the goods yard. In fine weather she had taken Trautchen with her, when it was raining the little one had stayed at home.

As a result the supervision Trautchen received was less than a four year old needed and less than my mother was happy with. At some stage Trautchen must have been drinking water from the tap without it had been boiled or she had come into contact with a deadly germ somewhere else. She contracted either typhus or dysentery and died two weeks later in a hospital just across the road. The diagnosis was vague, because there was no doctor of any kind at the hospital. My mother had lost all will to live, but she had to go on living for the sake of Eka.

I must have read the words on the card a dozen times. Already after reading them the first time, I knew what I had to do. I would fetch my mother and Eka to the West. Either we would make it, or we would all perish. At that moment I would have accepted either option.

That evening I showed my father the postcard from my mother. His reaction was a mixture of grief and elation; grief about Trautchen and elation about the possibility of linking up with the rest of the family. He rejected outright the thought of me going to Berlin. Times were such in the Russian sector of Germany that it was unwise for a young woman to travel to Berlin and back. There was no sense in one member of the family sacrificing herself for the others. I explained to him that I had no intention of sacrificing myself. I was very blunt and told him that, in his emaciated condition, he would be the most unsuitable candidate for the job. Matters were now too serious, to be concerned about paying compliments to each other. I might only just have turned nineteen, but I had matured far beyond my years. However obedient I was as a child, I was now as stubborn as the proverbial mule.

Whether he liked it or not, it was true; my father was physically too weak to endure the hardships of such a journey. I also believed that he was not as canny or as resourceful as I had become on my travels in eastern Germany. His experiences had not taken him further than the western front and West Germany. Above all, he was timid and over-careful by nature. I boldly put all those points before him. In the end, very reluctantly, he relented and gave me his blessing to go to Berlin. I would go and bring Eka and my mother back and leave Trautchen to sleep on in the cemetery. Our living room had looked out onto the cemetery. She had loved that part of Berlin, as we all had.

The decision had been made; now I had to concentrate on the preparations. I handed in my notice, which resulted in the rest of my patients being transferred to another ward. On paper, the Red Cross in Germany was at that time still a Nazi organisation. There was a swastika on the badge, which I wore pinned to my uniform. Therefore, I had to be 'denazified', a process which took place within the vast camp of Munsterlager. Admittedly the camp was not that far away from Lüneburg, but the back-log, with which the British authorities had to deal, was enormous. I spent nearly six weeks in that camp. Always trying to think positively, I spent a part of that time trying to learn some Russian. I figured that that decision might make the difference between luck and misfortune on my journey.

I had been very friendly with the pharmacist, Irene Gäbler, at our hospital. Irene was in her mid-twenties. When she heard of my plans, she decided to come as well. Her home was in Frankfurt on the Oder, well to the east of Berlin. All her family and friends lived there, and she had no intention of returning to the west. Apparently her parents had kept their house and garden. For her, things could only get better. True, the area would become East Germany, but she would live comfortably.

My situation was rather different. The property we owned in Treptow was in the province of Pommern. Not only did Pommern now belong to Poland, but the Poles had expelled all Germans, in order to avoid future unrest in the area. They had learned from the history of the Polish Corridor, the piece of land which Germany had lost to Poland after the First World War. As long as Poles and Germans had lived together there, they had quarrelled. This was now supposed to be the perfect and permanent solution and I had resigned myself to that. Some Germans had lost their houses in bombing raids; others lost their property in the redefining of frontiers. A price had to be paid for the cruel war which Germany had started.

Naturally, I was pleased that I would have company on my journey to Berlin. I hoped to be with my family on the return journey. I had no civilian clothes. So I packed a small bag and travelled in my uniform to Munsterlager. I was given a bed in a large dormitory, was fed in a soup kitchen and was finally called for an interview with a British major. He was pleased not to have to send for an interpreter and began by asking a list of questions, the answers to which he noted down on a form.

Finally he leaned back and told me that something in my replies did not add up. I had answered every question truthfully and was now worried that things were not going according to plan. He started at the beginning, picking out things he wanted me to confirm. "You have been a member of the Hitler Youth. You were in the *Arbeitsdienst* (Labour Service). I don't count the Red Cross. That should not have been a reason why they sent you here, whether it was affiliated to the Party or not. Now we go on. You intend to head back to Berlin. I understand you have started to learn Russian here. You tell me you want to fetch your mother. How do I know what you are going there for? It must be very unusual for a girl your age to want to go back into the Russian sector. All the borders are closed. There is no train to Berlin, no mail, no public transport through the city centre." He looked at me, baffled. Is some organisation protecting you or putting you up in East Germany?"

"No, Sir. I can only say I have answered your questions truthfully. It surprises me, though, that you put so much weight onto a few months of singing and camping in the Hitler Youth, and that at the age of eleven. I am not sure what you think I am going to Berlin for. Do you think I am a spy? This is something you have not asked me, so I'll tell you of my own free will. I am not a spy. As you know I have travelled a lot in the east. I have yet to meet a Soviet soldier. I hope I never will, but you never know, and that is why I've learned some Russian phrases. Sometimes, a few friendly words in a person's own language will make a soldier smile instead of frown." The major laughed, and added, "Just like you've done now." Still smiling, he signed the form, and another, which he then handed to me. It had his name on it and a large rubber stamp. That would get me anywhere in the western sector.

I was free to go. Without public transport all I could do was sit on the verge of the road and hope for a lift. A hay cart came along. I hopped on and sat beside the driver. He took me to the next town where I thanked him, walked to the station and caught a train to Lüneburg.

My friend Irene, the pharmacist, thought I had gone missing, as did my father. She did not have to endure a stay at Munsterlager, she did not belong to the Red Cross or the *Hitler Youth*. Irene would prove a true friend and companion on the journey ahead and I would support her to the best of my ability. I had my nurses' coat died black, collected a few necessities in a bundle and organised two loaves of bread to give to a guide at the border. He would take us through some woodland into East Germany. I could not communicate with my mother. My visit would be a complete surprise to her, for she neither knew that one of her post cards had been handed to me, nor would she have known what my reaction had been - or would she?

Now that everything had been prepared for the journey, I wanted to be off. I said good-bye to my father and my friends and patients and then, on the last night before we left, lay tossing and turning in a bed which Irene had organised in the pharmacy. Trautchen kept coming into my mind, wanting a cuddle or her favourite semolina pudding. I could not lie down any longer and got up to walk the corridors of the hospital and finally the empty street outside. It was a beautiful part of Lüneburg. My mother would grow to like it as well. Only Trautchen would not have the opportunity to enjoy it and once more I felt the tears begin to well up in my eyes. When I returned to the pharmacy, way up on the top floor of the hospital, it was still dark. Irene had already stacked our beds away and was ready to leave. There was a train to Göttingen around five in the morning which we wanted to catch. We shouldered our rucksacks, put black scarves on our heads and took one last look at our place of work, which held many happy memories. Then we closed the door to the pharmacy and closed another chapter in both our lives.

7.

The guide met us at Göttingen station where we jumped down from an open goods wagon. He was there with his wife and we paid our dues to her. Between them they had three ancient bicycles in good working order on which he, Irene and I would propel ourselves to the vicinity of the border. His wife soon left us. She had obviously only helped with the bicycles. We identified ourselves, but asked no questions as was requested for his safety. In a country with no postal service or telephone you just ask a man who knew a man who happened to be a frontier guide. I had obtained my information about a guide at the camp in Munsterlager where any information concerning the movements between East and West was readily available, as was the charge for any such services. I cannot remember for how long we cycled because we stopped for a longish break at midday, but by dusk we had arrived at some unmade lane. There, another stranger was waiting and said no more than pass the time of day. He took and locked the guide's bike within the yard of a nearby house and walked off with the other two bicycles. We followed the guide down the lane into a copse and woodland. Our progress was slow as we often stopped when listening to unusual noises.

In open country we would have left silhouettes on the skyline. In the woods there was only the sound of cracking timber which could have given us away. The guide knew exactly where a given Soviet patrol would operate, as though they had handed him a timetable of their movements. To us, knowing all this was well worth the two loaves I had brought for him. Incidentally, Irene had handed his wife some sausages as well. We then simply followed him like sheep. When we finally came out into a clearing, he stopped and said, "You are now in East Germany."

He showed us the track which led to Ebergötzen, some more trees, but no more woods. We had studied and memorised the map of the area so well, and Irene had this map in her rucksack, so that was all the guidance we needed in order to find our way. For my benefit, since he knew that I hoped to return, he volunteered more information. "This woodland behind us is going to be cleared very soon. The Russians want better vision. So don't rely on finding a way through here in a month's time." We shook hands and he left us.

The general plan was to avoid getting into towns and cities if possible. Only if the opportunity arose to go safely to a railway station, would we change our plan. We had brought food for a couple of days. We were, therefore, relying on generous farmers and the gift of a hot meal now and then. Money was worthless, and we had no opportunity to get a ration-book in East Germany. As regards accommodation, we were self-sufficient and would sleep under the stars. We both knew that a hundred and one things would change our minds, very bad weather, getting separated or getting caught, to name but a few. We would live from one day to the next and each day move that bit closer to Berlin. There were also days when we moved further away from that city simply because a certain place promised a more rapid advance a day later. We figured that we had embarked on a 250 to 300 kilometre journey. There was a much shorter way via Helmstedt, but the chances of crossing there were said to be nil.

A train journey was certainly a very attractive proposition to us, but it had to be safe, safe from the point of view of the attention of Russian soldiers. I don't remember paying for a ticket on any train. They were primarily used to transport Soviet army personnel. If you were lucky, you slipped into the last coach of a train which was often empty of passengers. Soviet soldiers usually congregated in the middle of the train. Our greatest fear was that of hearing a soldier call, "*Frau komm` mit*." (Woman, come with me.) That would have been followed by the iron grip of a hand on the woman's arm from which there was no escape. To steer clear of being molested, we always tried to find out in advance where the Russians had a camp or garrison, and where they might go in the evenings after their issue of vodka. As time went on, we witnessed several fights over girls and there was usually a bloody end to those brawls. In comparison, officers were extremely civilised in that respect and were quite ready to break up a brawl, even if they had to administer rough justice to their own troops.

I remember one train journey, quite early in our travels, where a local train sat in a siding. Locals told us that we should board the train from the other side. "Don't use the platform at all," they warned. We did as we were told and climbed into the last coach. Half an hour later the train pulled out. It was supposed to head north-east to the nearest bigger town. Instead the train went due east, but before we reached any town, the train slowed down and our coach stopped at a level crossing. Some twenty Soviet officers tried to get in. Our only thought was to get out - as fast as possible. In the confusion I dropped several things. Red in the face, I watched two officers recover the articles and politely hand them to me. I smiled and thanked them - in Russian. They were delighted and gave each of us an apple and an orange. At the time fear must have been written all over my face, but memories like this have given me much pleasure and restored my confidence in human kindness. On that occasion we quickly hurried off to anywhere as long as it was to a built-up area. We had again travelled in the wrong direction and it was quite impossible to judge the exact length of our journey. All I know is that it took us about two weeks to get to Berlin and three or four days to get back to Lüneburg and yet that time was packed so full of impressions that it seemed more like two or three months than two or three weeks.

Food need not have worried us. When we asked we were always given something, but it was rarely hot food, more likely a couple of apples, or something else out of the garden, or occasionally some stale rolls before the baker closed his shop for the day. It made no difference whether we had made our request around lunch or tea time or later in the evening. Food was short and we knew it and appreciated receiving whatever it was. I remember one day we stopped at a cluster of greenhouses where tomatoes had been harvested. There were now only tiny ones left on the dried up plants. The owner told us to help ourselves and bed down in one of the glasshouses if we wished. He also recommended filling our pockets before we left in the morning. Those were the little surprises we encountered which I still remember.

We walked long distances, met many friendly people on the way and the weather was kind to us. Most of the walking was done at dusk or after dark. One farmer offered to take us in his horse-drawn cart to the village station. He swore that from there it would only be fifteen minutes by train to Magdeburg, which was more than half way to Berlin. More important still, the train sat at the local station all night and left at six in the morning almost empty. In Magdeburg the Berlin express train would be waiting. It all sounded like a fairy tale.

The farmer knew what was worrying us. Would the express train be full or half empty? It would certainly not be empty. We were right there, but could we not slip into the guard's van and hide amongst the luggage or whatever was usually piled up there? He told us about the mirror boxes underneath the guard's van. Those boxes had been fitted especially for the conveyance of mirrors and glass. The shelves could be pulled out and pushed to the back. Then one of us would fit in there. We would have to travel on different days perhaps. There would not be a second mirror box. In the end we decided to accept the offer of a lift in the cart and to take the slow train to Magdeburg. Whilst on that train we had time to consider our next option. It was too good a suggestion to discard without serious thought.

Imagine stepping into an express train and travelling all the way to Berlin - even if the luxury compartment was exchanged for a mirror box!

Magdeburg station was crowded, the very conditions we had so far tried to avoid. We tightened our head scarves and shuffled forward in a slightly bent posture. From a distance we may have looked elderly, but close up we could not hide the smooth skin, the full lips and the big eyes of our young faces. At all costs we had to steer clear of any military presence. On a different platform our express train was waiting... and so was a large crowd of Soviet troops. We hurried to the guard's van. Even that activity was not in keeping with the likely behaviour of two elderly women. All precautions seemed to have been abandoned.

A look into the guard's van satisfied us that it was empty, except for some sacks piled one on top of the other. Irene climbed in. We had already discovered the mirror box. I busied myself sorting out the timber frames inside, pushed my rucksack in and I doubled up in the rest of the available space. I reached for one of the straps of the rucksack, fed it through an iron ring in the trap door and pulled it shut. I could hear the noise outside. No-one could see me. Anyone passing might see a bit of strap on the box below the guard's van, but who, when starting on a long rail journey, would bother about a piece of strap? The travellers' eyes, I figured, would all focus on doors and windows and where they could find an empty seat. I thought Irene and I had made the perfect decision when we boarded the train.

Already in Lüneburg we had contemplated the possibility of being separated on the journey, that one was caught but not the other, or that both were caught and ended up in different places. We agreed that each should pursue her own objective, if necessary on her own. Coming to the aid of the other would only result in both of us failing to reach our goals. We had to accept that failure was quite likely, but not by either of us trying to be heroic. That attitude would have achieved nothing. So far everything had gone so well that we were perhaps a little too casual on the last lap of our journey.

The train left on time and arrived in Berlin on time. The arrangement was that we would wait a while until all the passengers had disembarked. We knew the same train would return to Magdeburg but not for a couple of hours. We would have plenty of time to extricate ourselves – Irene from behind the sacks in the guard's van and I from the mirror box. I opened the flap when all was quiet. There was no-one about. I crawled out and recovered my rucksack. There was no sign of Irene, not in the guard's van and not on the platform. I called softly and then louder. There was no reply. I just could not give up lightly. At the end of the platform was a pile of boxes and parcels. I made myself sitting room amongst them and spent the remainder of the day wondering where Irene had gone. It was so unlike her to leave without a word, whether under duress or otherwise. She had known where I was and that I would hear her once she was out on the platform. Towards the evening it became clear that I had to leave the station. I had no other option. It would have been dangerous to spend the night on the platform. As darkness approached I made my way into the city. I could only think that Irene had befriended some railway guard. He might have suggested that she should jump off before the train came to a halt and quickly race up the stairs. She may well have wanted to hide somewhere to let me know that she was safe, but she did not have the opportunity.

I had only known Irene for about a year, but we had grown very fond of each other. Above all, we had shared the hard times. When she had obtained a piece of margarine and I had been able to get hold of a few extra potatoes, then we treated ourselves to fried potatoes, all prepared and cooked on a Bunsen burner in the pharmacy. When a certain medication was in short supply for one of my patients, Irene would go out of her way to obtain some of it. It is strange, though, that I do not recall meeting her socially for a hike in the heath-land surrounding Lüneburg or for a chat about our families. I only knew that she was going to Frankfurt on the Oder, but she knew my address. It therefore followed that any contact had to be initiated by her and it was.

About a year later when postal services had resumed, I received a letter from Irene. Inside was a photo of herself, her husband and a small baby in her arms. The writing was of little help to me in solving the mystery of her disappearance. She started off by saying that she had already written several times, but had received no reply from me. Half the first sheet of paper had been blacked out. The rest had been so heavily censored that all I gleaned from the letter was that she had married a childhood friend and they had had a baby. Her address on the letter and on the back of the envelope had also been heavily blacked out. I could not write to her. We never heard from each other again. Someone was determined that Irene would have no contact with anyone in the West.

In later life my son tried to establish her whereabouts, but without success. I had moved a long way away. She may have done the same. I did not know her married name, she did not know mine. It was not unusual that war-time friendships, forged strong in necessity or adversity, were quickly lost. I am pleased that I still have her picture. For all I know she will still have mine.

We had arrived beside a Berlin station which I had frequented when engaged in competitive rowing. As I moved on I recognised nothing. We had travelled as far as the track had been usable. What followed were mountains of rubble. Sometimes a building façade was still standing. More often I now found hills and valleys of broken brick and concrete. Some of the main streets had a narrow channel cleared for military vehicles to move in single file. The task of systematic clearance by the women of Berlin had not yet started in earnest.

It was dark now. I could see no human being anywhere. People here lived in cellars underneath the piles of rubble. I thought it best to creep into a hole in the rubble myself and wait for the dawn. In conditions like that, when there is not much to see, other senses take over. I spread my rubber sheet out, wrapped myself in my overcoat and stretched out on a hard 'bed'. I must have dreamt that I was in Berlin again, for I saw the boats lined up on the banks of the Wannsee. I heard the starting whistle quite clearly and then the roar of applause when we reached the finishing line. It was good to be back in the city with its large green belts of parks and forests, and tall houses as well. Slums were part of the picture too. For most Berliners the search for a home began there. I dozed.

Suddenly I was wide awake. Someone, awake like me, was playing the mouth-organ not far from where I had bedded down. I knew the tune well. The song told the story of the two rivers which would always flow through Berlin, no matter what happened to the city. Whether the words had been written with this chaos in mind is doubtful.

I had not eaten all day, and I fancied my chances of asking for a piece of bread from the mouth-organ player. I packed up all my belongings and started moving towards the player. It was a woman. Her two children asleep, she had ventured outside for some fresh air and the soothing sound of her own music. She asked me into her 'home', a small place with everything at hand. She did not enquire whether I was hungry. She simply put a plate of hot potato soup in front of me and a piece of dry bread to go with it. I cannot remember a meal having tasted so good before or since. She then offered me her bed for the rest of the night and when I protested, she said she would go out and go on playing anyway. I did not argue any more but dropped onto her bed to resume my pleasant dreams. I was, indeed, back in Berlin and found the people so friendly and helpful that I vowed there and then to be back in the city one day, not to see all the architectural transformations, but to be with the people once again.

I slept until almost midday and then made a hasty departure. The Good Samaritan had no address and the woman did not know where she might be next week or next year, but she assured me, she would still be in Berlin. I made her laugh when I said that, with her accent, people would not want her anywhere else. She insisted on giving me another piece of bread. She also explained that by heading north along the outskirts, and then east, I would avoid the impenetrable city. I would also find some of the electric trains running outside the city centre. This information proved to be very helpful.

I spent the rest of that day and the following one clambering through rubble and walking between stations where the tracks were being repaired. Finally, I emerged at the station *Prenzlauer Berg* to find the good old tram No 71 waiting to take me home. As I had done hundreds of times, I alighted at our block of flats - at the cemetery gates to be precise - and started walking towards our front door. A cold shiver ran down my back at the thought that Trautchen might be watching me from inside the cemetery.

In just a few minutes I was inside the house, up the stairs and ringing the familiar bell. I was leaning against the wall panting when I heard my mother call from inside: "Who is it?" My answer was even briefer. "It's me." How many variations are there in the pronunciation of two words? It would appear a mother does not need more than two words to recognise her child and yet, she hesitated before opening the door. Some things you just cannot believe, however much the facts have convinced you to the contrary. Then the door was flung open. We were in each other's arms and the tears expressed what words were inadequate to achieve. They were tears of sorrow at the loss of my little sister, of joy at the reunion and of hope that together we would fight for a new life and a better future. Together we would make it.

Silently Eka had crept up on us. I let go of my mother and took Eka in my arms, and we wiped each other's tears away. Then the door was closed, locked from the inside and the chain replaced. It was a formality because if certain individuals had really wanted to get in they would have broken the door down. Inside our flat there were other people - people I did not know. I do not think I even asked about them. I presumed they were bombed out and had been accommodated in our flat. I would, in any case, not be staying long enough to become acquainted. We introduced each other and shook hands; that was all. My mother, Eka and I then moved into my mother's bedroom for privacy.

I had made all the plans and my mother agreed without protest. We would leave that night and take the tram and the electric train for as far as they operated in the desired direction. Then we would make for the station at which I had arrived in the city. Whilst waiting for Irene to turn up, I had made a valuable discovery. On a different platform hundreds of elderly or disabled women were waiting for a goods train to take them to West Germany. They would not have been an asset to the Soviet rebuilding programme; the British sector, no doubt, would have had little use for them either, but for my family those goods trains represented a chance. There was supposed to be one train leaving for the West every afternoon. No-one knew for how long. We could only hope to be in time and take what we could carry. My mother started packing immediately.

She was very worried she might have to return to the flat. Maybe there would be no more trains leaving. Maybe the Russians would refuse to let us travel on the train. Having deserted her job, there would then be very serious repercussions. I tried to put her mind at rest, but every now and then the lurking fear returned. Except for a ground sheet, my rucksack was empty, intentionally. Knowing how many things we were short of in Lüneburg, I wanted to bring back with me as many useful items as possible. My mother packed three rucksacks and two pieces of hand luggage. I had told her that we owned nothing in our new flat in Lüneburg. My father had one blanket and a pillow and that belonged to the landlady.

My mother started worrying again. Would the landlady let her and Eka stay in that room as well? I told my mother that I had asked her before I left Lüneburg. "The answer was yes." With that many rooms she would have had to put up even larger families than ours.

My mother had news for me as well. My piano teacher had called on her. She had arrived from her studio in her high-heeled shoes. I could hardly believe it. "What did she want?" I asked.

"She enquired after you," my mother said. I sat there on my mother's bed trying to picture the incident. I felt very honoured. This lady, formerly a concert pianist and once a teacher of pupils like the daughter of our ambassador to Canada, had called on my mother to find out how I was. It is true that she would have had a telephone, but no-one else did in the area. She could learn nothing from that. If you wanted to find out anything you had to use your two feet – and she had done just that.

"Did she say anything about the people she was sheltering behind her house?" I asked.

My mother stopped her packing and sat down beside me. She had forgotten to ask my piano teacher about those people because, soon after my mother arrived in Berlin, she heard from another source that my teacher's friends had left Berlin. They had left from a collecting point at the city centre. Once hostilities had ceased, they must have been all right, although little is generally known about individuals. That was my mother's version of those events. It all sounded very vague to me.

I went to the living room, leaving my mother to continue her packing. It was the only room which had a view of the tram lines and the cemetery beyond. In fact, none of the windows looked out onto the side of the house with the front door. That fact became my salvation within the next few minutes. I had opened the window and looked across to where Trautchen might have been buried. My mother had advised me not to go there, because beside the cemetery were Russian billets and officers' quarters. It was the most sought-after part of our suburb and I had reluctantly agreed to stay indoors. Deep in thought, leaning on the window sill, I suddenly heard the dreaded call: "*Frau, komm` mit.*" My first reaction was to close the window. I saw the soldier running towards our house. Then I fled to my mother's bedroom. My mother locked me into the wardrobe, a hiding place which had frequently been used by her and my sister. My mother watched what happened next. Not knowing the geography of the flats, the soldier had stormed into the wrong front entrance. He could not find me and I made doubly sure that he would not. It was certainly wise to leave the area as soon as possible.

We used up what food there was, had a good meal and packed up the rest for the journey. My mother had packed something of everything. We also found a few things for me to wear, so that I could change from the nurses' uniform. There was a skirt belonging to my mother and my father's pullover. I kept the black coat and scarf which had served me so well on the outward journey. I stuffed my pockets full of leather straps and short pieces of rope because they might come in useful, although it was impossible to predict what we would need.

Shortly before we left, one of my aunts arrived. She had taken some trouble over her appearance with make-up - to create an impression of age and disease with good effect! She gave us some make-up, some items which might come in handy on our journey. My mother handed her the key of the flat. Maybe one day she could send us on a few more of our belongings.

At dusk my mother looked out of the window. Everything was quiet. No Germans in their right minds would have walked the streets. Most of the soldiers were having their evening meal, and in ten minutes the tram was expected to stop at the cemetery gates. We said good-bye to the other occupants in our flat, hugged my aunt and made our way to the cemetery gates. Waiting for the tram was agony. My mother had grasped the iron bars of the cemetery gate and was sobbing. To leave Trautchen, her little angel, behind all on her own, was more than she could bear. If only she had put up with those horrible relations in Lüneburg and stayed a little longer in their flat, if only she had waited for me to return from my nursing course as had been arranged instead of returning to her beloved flat in Berlin... I gently pulled her away from the cemetery gates and reminded her that Trautchen was no longer in the cemetery. Anyone as innocent as her would now be watching and praying for her mother from Heaven.

The tram clanked over the points and came to a halt. As was the procedure from now on, I let my mother and Eka climb in first, handed them the five pieces of luggage, and then boarded myself. How do you say good-bye to your home? I was convinced I would never see it again, but I thought I had learned something else that night; people are far more important than bricks and mortar. A home is, after all, only the shell in which people live. It is the people who make the shell a 'home', who make it happy or otherwise, who bring joy or grief.

Presently we transferred to the electric train and took that until it came to a halt just short of the track which, at this point, was bent upwards in ghostly shapes of twisted metal. We started walking. No-one grumbled about their load or the conditions of the streets. There came the moment when we could walk no further. We were all too tired to carry on and found ourselves a place to sleep, well hidden and as soft as possible. No-one played the mouth-organ for us, and I am sure no-one slept.

The following day we walked parallel to the river Havel towards Wannsee station. I remember about half a dozen tracks, all culminating in as many platforms. It was chilly out, and we made for the large waiting room at the end of one of the platforms. That may not have been a wise decision, for the platform next to us was already filling with elderly women, many of them limping or disabled in some way. We made enquiries and were told that this was the platform from which the 'unwanted' would be travelling to the West.

The waiting room was not crowded. There was only one chair and I let my mother sit on it. All other seating facilities must have been used for firewood during the previous winter. Within an hour about twenty people had joined us. We asked if they knew when the train would leave and were told in three hours time and then trouble arrived in the shape of a Soviet guard. He surveyed the scene and, in sign language, told my mother to get off the chair and let me sit on it. We did not seek an argument with him. My mother stood up and I sat down. There was peace for a few minutes, but he kept his eye on us. After another hour or so he wanted the chair to be brought to the front, near where he sat on a table. I was to sit there under his gaze. We obliged, my mother staring at me and my eyes fixed on the ground.

At the back of the room someone fainted, or made it look that way. The soldier immediately moved over to see what had happened. Within seconds we had grabbed our belongings, fled outside and into the area of trees and bushes beyond. "That was a lucky escape," my mother panted. I counted our belongings several times, although, had I left a rucksack in the waiting room, I would not have gone back to retrieve it. We now approached the platform of waiting people from another direction, every now and then glancing across at the waiting room, to make sure the soldier was not looking out for us. All was quiet.

There were so many people waiting for that train now, that we believed only half of them would have found space inside the coaches. I was worried. It would be the same tomorrow... if there was a train. We were so tightly packed, standing there; the least commotion would have spilled some of the people onto the track. To keep out of sight of the Soviet guard, we had joined the crowd at the wrong side of the platform. There was no way we could have pushed ourselves from the back to the front. My mother was already in tears, fearing the worst. We agreed though that if she could get in with Eka, she should do so. I would somehow follow her the next day with the luggage. She did not like the arrangement but finally agreed; that might have been the only solution to our problem.

When the time came, the engine backed some twenty cattle trucks beside the platform. Two women fell off the concrete edge onto the track. Helping hands pulled them up to safety, just in time. Women shouted, children screamed. The Soviet guard shouted in Russian through a megaphone. No one understood. The engine driver continued backing the long snaking line of trucks to the end of the platform and there it stopped. The sliding doors were already open; the crowd surged forward and into the trucks like animals. We, at the back, stood little chance of boarding. If all had gone well in the waiting room, we would have been in the front, although the chance of being pushed over the edge might have deterred us. We now had to do the best we could.

Finally the trucks were full, standing room only of course. People even stood on their luggage to conserve space. There was over half an hour to go before the train was due to leave. All those who had given up hope of boarding, were already leaving the platform. I had a very quick word with my mother. I then jumped up onto the edge of the opening and pushed the crowd back another foot to loud screams of protest. I pulled my mother in beside me, jumped out, helped Eka in to take my place and slid the doors of the wagon shut from the outside. I could tell my mother was very unhappy about my solution. The last I heard was my mother pleading for me to try and find somewhere on the train, even if it meant leaving luggage on the platform. Now the doors were closed. Casualties caused by suffocation were a real possibility, but I am sure no one would have wanted to get out again.

I stood on the platform with three rucksacks and two bags like 'hold-alls'. I eyed the back of the wagon with its rails, iron rings and metal grips. I roped the bags onto the buffers, strapped the rucksacks securely to metal handholds, cables and rings and then settled myself down on top of the bags with the rucksacks dangling above and beside me. The 'dangling' was soon stopped with leather straps as these were used to hold the whole creation solidly together. Lastly, I strapped myself in, very securely with belts and ropes. My activities and my perch were even out of sight of the waiting room and the Soviet guard. As far as I was concerned, the train could now leave.

It left exactly on time and, warmly wrapped up in my coat, the scarf securely knotted, I saw the platform pass beside me and the stones beneath me. I knew the draught would be minimal close behind the wagon. It would pass each side of me like a tornado, though. I hoped I was right... and that I would not slide off. To this day, when seeing goods-trains and their buffers, I look at them with great respect.

The town on the western edge of the Soviet zone, towards which the train was steaming, was called Heiligenstadt (Holy Town). I hoped the town would live up to its name. That journey lasted several hours with brief stops of rest for the engine and covered a distance of nearly 300 kilometres including diversions to take account of damaged tracks. At the time my main concern was to stay on the buffers. It was the most memorable journey I had made.

Finally, the train drew to a halt. We had arrived! It would take me some time to extricate myself from my seat on the buffers. Meanwhile the sliding doors had been opened. The people jumped and fell out and many stayed on the ground gasping for fresh air. My mother, as yet unaware of my close proximity, had survived the ordeal as well. At one point I called to her. She was overcome with joy when she saw me and took me in her arms. We celebrated the happy event with a sip each out of her water bottle. She then helped me to untie the luggage. There was less pressure to hurry, but we still had a walk of several kilometres ahead of us, as well as coming under the scrutiny of three Soviet border guards at intervals of about a hundred metres. That came as news to us. I could never understand why there were three, unless each had a different aspect to check.

We joined the queue moving towards Friedland, another aptly named place (Land of Peace). This village was just within the British zone of occupation. When we saw the first Soviet checkpoint in the distance, my mother and I used eye-shadow to paint some wrinkles on our faces. To that we added a few red spots with a piece of my aunt's lipstick to simulate the symptoms of some unpleasant medical condition or disease. I am afraid our efforts could not be compared with my aunt's skills! Nor did we have a mirror. Whatever my mother did to me, and I to her, had to suffice. To the make-up I added a limp and my mother developed one shoulder alarmingly higher than the other. Eka's main task was to try and suppress her own laughter!

Gradually the crowd started to form a single line. They were mostly women and children, with only the occasional elderly man. There were certainly no young men. Suddenly I noticed that everyone was holding some form or piece of paper, presumably to hand to the guard. I asked the woman in front of me about the meaning of the sheet of paper.

"We're supposed to hand in doctors' certificates to say what we're suffering from. They should also say how old we are."

"Well," I said, "We've nothing like that. What do we do?"

She reached into her bag for a similar sheet of paper to her own. "Here, you can have that." I turned it over a couple of times.

"But this is a gas bill!" I exclaimed.

"It hasn't even been paid," laughed the woman. "None of these Russians speak a word of German, and we don't speak Russian. I haven't got a doctor's certificate either, and if you look down the line, nobody has." I turned round to check behind me.

A woman who had overheard our conversation showed me a letter from her husband, a prisoner-of-war in the American Sector. She was going to present that. "At the end of the day," she explained, "the border guards have to hand in so many pieces of paper against so many bodies delivered. You work it out for yourself. There aren't enough doctors left in Berlin to waste their time writing something which no-one can read."

When it was my turn, I handed over my gas bill. He seemed to be quite satisfied. The trouble started when there was no piece of paper for my mother and Eka. The woman in front of me was still sorting her rucksack. She quickly reached into her bag and pulled out more bills to give me. They had been paid, but they were dated 1932. Now everything was in order. He bowed as if to wish us a happy crossing and off we went. We owed so much to that woman who helped us with the 'documentation' that we gave her some of our possessions which I had brought from Berlin.

The second border guard came into sight. He started on about paper and I pointed in the direction of his colleague who had just wished us a happy crossing. He had taken all our papers. We had none left. I tried to explain in my broken Russian and in sign language but he only became increasingly exasperated with us. Eventually we were allowed to proceed. As long as that was westwards, I did not mind.

I dreaded what might transpire with the third border guard. I need not have worried. He was fast asleep, bent over his desk. The long queue tiptoed quietly past his hut. Once out of earshot we began our celebrations. We dipped into water bottles with a piece of rag and cleaned our faces. We shared our last pieces of food. We simply lay in the grass to rest from carrying our packs for so long.

Those are memories of the earliest times of occupation. Every child and adult in 'East Germany', or, as they say, 'New Federal Provinces', would now learn to speak Russian. In fifty years time they may all speak English. One day they might even be one people living in one country. Whether the differences that have been forged through decades of separation will ever be eliminated or reduced, remains to be seen. When I had safely brought my mother and Eka to West Germany, no-one at home or abroad could envisage the prospects of a united Germany and, in any case, on this journey we were not in the mood for speculations on that scale. We just wanted to get to our destination, eat when we were hungry and sleep when we were tired.

After our deserved rest, we shouldered our rucksacks again. There in the distance we could already make out the confines of the refugee camp of Friedland. We were now within the British zone of occupation. In little groups we reached the gates and were directed to the wash-houses and supplied with powders and liquids to rid ourselves of lice and fleas. There was no need to be squeamish; we all had them. After a long wash, we dropped our old unwanted clothes into a bin. The rest was all disinfected and put back on again.

We then received a bowl of soup, rich in vegetables and meat, and we could ask for a second helping! Unfortunately, we had to leave the following morning, when the place would be prepared for the next intake. I fear there were not many more to come. We seemed to have hit on exactly the right time for our journey. A few days earlier and our preparations might not have stood up to the increased scrutiny. A few days later and it would have been too late for many reasons. There may not have been fuel for the railway engine, the British may have got fed up with the influx of useless people or the Soviets might have found room for them within their own territory.

Presently we were lying on the grass enjoying the evening. Now there was plenty of time to talk and we learned from fellow Germans where they had come from and where they were going, but we did not have to ask, "Why?" They all had feared deportation to places from which there was no return, with or without reason and, with very few exceptions, they were all women and children. They all arrived in West Germany having left their homes in East Germany and all they now owned was what lay beside them in the grass.

8.

After leaving the camp we made for the main line station in Göttingen. There were still no passenger trains operating, but freight and coal trains stopped at every main station of the network. If you had to get from A to B, you could lie flat on top of a load of coal, or you could share the space inside a goods wagon with materials for construction sites. Such measures discouraged people from travelling by rail and that was the intention. You were meant to stay at home and work. That presupposed that your work-place was near your home. If it was not, it was time you moved to another flat or house. Fuel was not wasted in those days.

The only train scheduled for Lüneburg on that day was laden with coal. We climbed up and lay spread-eagled on top of the coal, clutching our belongings. Around lunchtime we arrived at our destination looking like miners emerging from their work at the coal face.

My father would be at work until five or six which meant we had to borrow a second key from the landlady. She was so horrified when she saw us, that she asked for the key to be washed before it was returned. It was surprising what a bath in a tin tub under the rafters could achieve. When all was finished we emerged in our room 'sparkling clean'. Our clothes were all washed and hung up on a line criss-crossing the rafters. That gave us a new idea. In our spare time we could take in washing and, if that service was paid for with cigarettes or coffee, we would have won the battle against poverty!

I could not wait until the evening. I had to tell my father the good news as soon as possible, whereupon he was given the afternoon off and sent home. The British sergeant at my father's workplace asked me to come in for a moment. He obviously wanted to talk to me about something. He still called me nurse. He probably did not know my name, nor would he have found it easy to pronounce. "I want to ask you something as well," I said, when we sat down opposite each other in the front room. "Who's first?" he smiled. I smiled as well and answered, "You go first; you've won the war."

"And we were told the Germans have no sense of humour."

"Don't believe all they tell you."

"Mine won't take long, anyway," he began. "I wanted to ask you if you would come to our dance on Saturday. Would you give me the honour?"

That kind of request I had not expected. The non-fraternisation policy was still in full force. I felt uncomfortable and voiced my reasons for being so slow in giving him a straightforward answer. I then remembered that this unit had been kind enough to give my father a job and that, if I refused, the sergeant would be quite justified in refusing my request as well. "When do I have to be here?" I asked. "Oh, any time after you've finished work."

"I no longer work. I have just come back from Berlin and it wasn't on a Luftwaffe passenger flight."

"All the more reason why we should have a good talk." He paused. "Anyway, thanks for accepting the invitation. Now, what did you want to ask me?"

I stammered around some sort of introduction to my request and then simply blurted out what was on my mind. "Would your soldiers, and there must be a dozen of them, need laundry facilities? My mother and I take in washing."

"Be great," he replied. "I'll pass on the message."

His reaction gave me more courage. "A week's bundle - ten cigarettes and either a piece of soap or a little bag of soda or washing powder. We can't buy either." I thought he smiled, but I cannot be sure now. "Give me a sec." He got up and disappeared only to return with two bundles of washing, the soldiers' numbers neatly written on each. "That's the first instalment," he said, "I'll have some more ready for you when you return this lot." In another bag he had forty cigarettes, a piece of soap and a whole carton of washing powder. He handed me that too. I protested at the generous payment, and that in advance, but he insisted. The interview was over, and I left.

I headed home in high spirits, and yet I was sorry to have missed my father's reunion with the rest of the family. We were all together now - nearly all. I felt a tear roll down my cheek, but I knew we, who were left, would survive.

The laundry business took off like a bomb. We had brought an electric iron from Berlin and were extra meticulous with shirts. Not being able to obtain wrapping paper, we carefully took off the old sheets in which the bundles had arrived and ironed them as well, before putting the clean laundry back into the old paper. For twenty cigarettes I bought myself a pair of new court shoes and for four cigarettes a second-hand dress. Not owning a mirror, I went all the way to the first shop window to study my reflection in the glass. I was pleased with it, the reflection and the dress!

In between ironing for soldiers, I went out to the job centre. Until there would be a currency reform, money would have limited value, but we did need it for our rations, rent and medical expenses. Luxuries could only be procured through barter. I felt I could do better than making 'Jumping Jacks' or washing clothes. There were plenty of jobs on offer but, although I had been reasonably well educated, I felt that I could never meet all the stipulated requirements. Office jobs were all taken up by local clerks and book keepers. My mother was a trained infant teacher. Those jobs were all filled as well or they no longer existed.

What could I do to improve my chances? I could speak English, but I could not type. All the jobs on offer with the occupation forces required typing if not shorthand as well. I would have to learn to type, a tall order if you had no chance of borrowing or buying a typewriter. I had no instrument to give music lessons. I had all but lost my skills in that direction anyway. Besides, I could not have expected any pupil to clamber through the loft to get to our room. There was also no further education available for people like me.

I accepted a job as a gardener. It was healthy outdoor work and yielded the odd cabbage beside my contribution to the general housekeeping. My mother kept the laundry going, and my father's work suited him given the limited opportunities and the fact that he was not very versatile. In our room were three single beds. I shared one with my sister, and the household items which we had brought from Berlin allowed us to live in relative comfort. My gardening job meant only temporary employment. Come the winter I would be paid off. So I kept looking out for alternatives.

The Saturday dance appointment approached. With new shoes and a respectable dress I looked forward to it. My father was on duty that evening as well to help prepare refreshments and clear up the aftermath. As we were ushered in, the cry went up, "Pop has brought his daughter." They all knew me by now because of our laundry business. I joined everyone in the crowded sitting room and my father disappeared into the kitchen. A soldier performed with gusto on a piano. It was a tune with endless verses. I asked the pianist what it was called. "The Lambeth Walk," he enlightened me. Also present, and dressed for the occasion, were the female cook, a cleaner and three or four girls

I did not know. Soon the dancing couples overflowed into the hall and dining room.

Belatedly the sergeant appeared and apologised for having been detained. He looked about him like a lost sheep, obviously deterred by the sight of this heaving humanity. "Would you like to dance?" he asked me. "Or shall we go and have a chat in the morning room?" I did not have to think twice.

"The morning room would be nice." I had no idea where that was, but he obviously knew the geography of the house. With access to the kitchen and the hall, the morning room looked out on to the back garden and the setting was beautiful.

The sergeant went out again and returned with a plate of sandwiches and a bottle of wine. From his breast pockets he picked two glasses which were about to fall out anyway, and we were set for a cosy little chat instead of performing contortions in the hall or sitting room. Even a keen dancer would have found little pleasure in moving in those surroundings.

He played the perfect host and then said, "Now it's your turn to tell me all about Berlin." At some stage he asked how the Russians had treated me.

"The Russians," I said, "at least some of them come from quite isolated regions. They try to adjust - try to jump from the eighteenth to the twentieth century. For hundreds of years they were suppressed themselves by Mongols and dictators in their own country. They think that's the way it is. Whoever is superior has the right to punish anyone inferior. I've seen how their soldiers treated German civilians with respect, and I've seen how Soviet officers treated their own men. It was often a matter of life and death, but nothing unpleasant has ever happened to me, although it could have done." I thought I had said enough. I was still learning about what was appropriate to say and what was not and, after all, I hardly knew this man.

I have often felt sorry for the ordinary Russians. The callous treatment they received in their own country, their forced Labour camps and the harsh temperatures in their easterly regions seemed to me to be impossible to bear. They had had a rough deal throughout history. I reached for another sandwich. It was time I changed the subject. "And where do you come from?"

"London," said the sergeant. For a second I wondered whether he would continue and tell me more about himself. He did. He took a deep breath. "I'm married with two children, one has forgotten me and the other's never met me."

"Oh... that must be hard for you. Tell me about them, if you want. I might only be nineteen and a German, but I've ended up listening to lots of soldiers' stories."

"Being German and nineteen might not encourage me to talk about my family, although I don't mind that either. I suppose having been a nurse has more to do with it. I feel I know you so well now that I could chat to you about anything." He smiled, and so did I.

"So, having been a nurse qualifies me to be an *agony aunt*." There was some truth in that statement. From the first day in the military hospital I was confronted daily with homesick soldiers and here was another one. As for *knowing me so well,* I thought he knew nothing about me, absolutely nothing. I listened to his story, and I felt for him, and only hoped that our brief time together had made him feel better, for a little while at least. He certainly was very good company without he knew me and without I knew him. He was to be demobbed in a month's time and his return to London could not have come too soon.

When it was time to go home, long before my father had finished his work, he thanked me for having come and apologised for not having danced with me. I looked up at him. "Which was more important to you, to talk or to dance?" I asked. "Both," he said sheepishly. "Come on then," I said. "We'll ask the piano player to add another verse to the Lambeth Walk!" We both enjoyed the outcome to the evening. It left me with plenty to think about on my short walk home.

A couple of days later, my father carried a dilapidated typewriter to our room. "The sergeant gave it to me for you to practise on," he told me and put it on the table. "You have to give it back when you've finished with it. He's obviously borrowed it." I was delighted. I must have mentioned to the sergeant that I needed typing skills for any office job, and he had done the rest. I asked my father to express my thanks to the sergeant when next he saw him. It was a very thoughtful thing to have done.

I started practising immediately. If you only typed with two fingers one would automatically assume that you had never been taught properly. Therefore, from day one, I laid my hands across the keyboard and allocated certain keys to each finger. I made very little progress and always slipped back into the bad two-finger habit. Being able to play the piano was no help either, but after two weeks or so I showed signs of improvement. I was impatient. That was all.

Another few weeks passed, and I thought that, with some tale about not having typed for a long time, I might persuade an employer that the speedy touch would soon come back to me. I would stay late in the office and go on with my practice sessions. I returned the old typewriter and tried my luck at the job centre again. I tried every day but there were no office jobs available. One day a kind office clerk spent a little more time with me and asked what else I could do besides typing. I told him that I could speak reasonably good English. "Now, that opens up a different field of opportunities," he smiled and gave me a piece of paper with an address written on it, as it happened in the road where we lived. "This is for a typist/interpreter." It sounded dreadfully posh.

"I have no qualifications, really," I stammered.

"Sit down there and think about it for a while," he suggested and went back to his desk.

I sat down and suddenly a little verse came to my mind, a verse my mother had written into my book of citations. "Never say, 'I can't' . . ." I jumped up and called the clerk. "I think I can do the job. I'll have a go, anyway." He smiled, waved good-bye from his desk and I left.

Although situated in my street which culminated in the main road south, it was a long walk to the address on the slip of paper. Presently I stood in front of a large, modern house with spacious offices downstairs and upstairs as well. I had no idea what the British army did behind those windows. Outside was a sign, No. 2 Purchase Section, a unit of Royal Engineers. I walked through the open door and was just going to knock on the first door inside, when a soldier came rushing out. "Go on in, somebody will be there to see you presently."

There were two desks and two chairs, a couple of filing cupboards and a pot plant on a stand. I looked out of the window; the road outside was dappled red, green and yellow with falling autumn leaves. The houses in the street were set back from the pavement; all had little front gardens, except the one I was waiting in. The would-be front garden had at some stage been concreted over and made into parking places, as though the house had been used for offices before. Towards the left was an unmanned level crossing which also marked the extent of the town's development in this direction. There were no more houses beyond the level crossing. The office was indeed a long way from the town centre.

Gone were the days when there was no postal service. Without that facility, no office could have functioned. It had, therefore, been a priority for whoever governed the country now to restore the infrastructure so that reconstruction could begin. The allies, together with the heads of some of the emerging new parties, worked on those projects. I turned round and noted that each desk in the room had a telephone. I also noted that, at the age of nineteen, I had actually never used a telephone before.

Involuntarily I began to giggle. At that moment the soldier, who had left the room, flung open the door again and noticed my amused expression. "And what's so funny?" he asked. He was no older than I was, and it seemed quite natural to talk to him in English. "I've been sent here to apply for a job," I said. "And I've just realised that I have never used a telephone. That is something I did not think I would have to learn."

"Sit down." He perched himself on top of one desk and invited me to do the same on the other desk. "Right," he went on, "I'll ring you now, as though I was the captain interviewing you, and you put your case and answer all the questions." I thought that was one way of learning to use a telephone. We sat opposite each other, he rang me and I picked up the receiver and looked at it curiously. "When it rings you're meant to put the damned thing to your ear... like this," he exploded, though not unkindly.

"I want to see where the words come out of the thing," I shouted back.

It was quite obvious that we had to start from the beginning again. Once the connection had been made and I understood the way the telephone worked, we had a pleasant conversation. He promised me the job, because I could telephone and speak English. As for the typing, the captain would have to decide. In the meantime we continued chatting, without the use of telephones, until the captain appeared. He was of medium height with short grey hair and a small grey moustache. I learned later that he was a veteran of the First World War. "Have you two got nothing to do?" he remarked as he passed us on his way to the door of his own office. Before putting his hand on the door handle, he stopped and turned round again, staring at me.

"Have I seen you before?" he mused. "And did I hear you speak English?"

"You haven't, Sir, and you did. I've been sent here by the Labour Exchange. I'm applying for a job as typist/interpreter, but, you see, my typing is a little slow." I was so pleased I had that lot off my chest.

"Never mind the typing," he shouted. "You can practice that any time. Consider yourself employed. Private Allthorpe will sort out the formalities."

"Is that him here?" I indicated the soldier who had just taught me to use a telephone.

"That's him." The captain took one last look at his new typist/ interpreter. Then his gaze fastened on to the private. Before the officer finally disappeared into his office I thought I heard him mumble, "That Allthorpe needs watching."

That was the end of my interview. One or two forms had to be filled in and signed. That was done. There were many questions I still wanted to ask, but I felt the young private had to get on with his own work now. I hoped I would be more useful in the months to come than I had been on that day. I took my leave, delighted that I had secured the job.

Once outside, instead of turning right for home, I turned left, went past the level crossing and turned into the heath-land beyond. It was such a nice afternoon, and God only knew, when I would have the opportunity again, to go skipping through the heathers, now in full bloom. Dozens of unmade roads wound their way through patches of short pines, birches and, of course, heathers. If it had not been for an old burnt-out tank or piece of artillery, one might never have believed that there had been a war and that so recently. Somewhere in that area Field Marshal Montgomery had accepted the surrender of the German forces. That was a piece of history which few people had witnessed, and which sat well in this landscape of colour and bloom. The war was over. I could not say it often enough. We were now working for a better future. Out of all this chaos and destruction a new Germany would emerge.

The office where I was about to start work arranged for factories to be repaired and building materials to be supplied to contractors, who would set about building and repairing houses and more factories. I was about to witness and become part of a tiny link in the chain of progress across the country. If a start were made, the rest would follow. These were, of course, the very beginnings of bringing the German economy back to life again. A small office in Lüneburg would not speed things up dramatically, but it would play its part. It was a step in the right direction and multiplied by hundreds of similar enterprises, it would certainly have an impact on the economy. Without strict controls, building materials would have landed on the black market, not helped the country as a whole – just a few dealers who would have lined their own pockets.

In those days it was quite difficult to find a person in Germany who could speak English. A school leaver a year older than I would have learned French as a first foreign language; anyone younger would not have attended school at all in the closing stages of the war and few, if any, would have attended English language courses whilst still at school as I had done.

I sensed that I would be content in this workplace. The captain was really more of a father figure; his bark was worse than his bite. The young soldiers, who had hardly seen any service, looked after their transport and rations. This left two middle-aged Germans and me who were answerable to the captain. He was responsible for the day to day running of the place.

Of the middle-aged Germans, one was an elderly, single woman called Miss Reiter. I shared an office with her. She was said to be a fully qualified foreign correspondent. She was accurate and fast on the typewriter in both German and English, but hated speaking in either language. If the telephone rang or someone in uniform entered the room, she would tread on my toes under the desk, the signal that she was too busy to attend to what could be 'safely left to me'. She seemed to be petrified of the telephone, and once told me that the British had a habit of talking Dutch on the phone - or even 'Double Dutch.' I think she lacked practice in spoken English. She had not done any for maybe twenty years. Now she had the opportunity but was too timid to take it.

The other middle-aged German, employed as an interpreter, was an ex-army officer. I felt he was rather self-opinionated. He reigned in a room of his own and gave us to understand that he singularly controlled the German factory owners and that he decided who was and who was not eligible for more materials. He was the person who had the knowledge about what each factory had produced or was capable of producing and when they had last been supplied. We two women saw very little of him. He seemed to spend a lot of time with the captain, after which he casually flung some notes across our desks as to what action was to be taken. The letters we then wrote were very short and to the point, with a copy retained for our files - the usual procedure in any office.

To be effective our office had to be enlarged. That happened after I had been there for a few months. Owing to the growing workload in our office, a group of Royal Engineers from the Headquarters in Hannover moved to Lüneburg. They were to assist with the management of our project. Not everyone was pleased about that. Our captain was agitated and furious. He expected to be pushed into a corner and be sidelined. The new boys would be more impatient, but would they be more efficient?

There were not so many of them as we expected, a major at the head of the team, a sergeant, a few lance corporals and two privates and that was all. Outside there appeared a Mercedes, an Audi, a Volkswagen, a five-ton Bedford lorry and a motorcycle. The general opinion was that the new boys would be happier with wheels under them than sitting in the office. Our cook, who up until then had only worked part-time, was now offered full-time employment. The German ex-army officer now had to take orders, not from the captain, but from the new sergeant who tolerated no arguments.

The major was a dapper, chain-smoking Scot. He was quite difficult to understand at times, and my female colleague made sure she was unavailable when he swept through the rooms in search of some piece of paper. If you showed him respect, he was always ready to crack a joke or have a good laugh, but if he thought anyone stared at his moustache for too long, he would ignore that person and stride past him, his chin held two inches higher than before. We, in the office, took note of the things happening around us, but were not really affected by the changes.

Things took a few days to sort themselves out. Unless marked private, Miss Reiter or I opened the mail, dealt with some simple replies and took the rest to the sergeant, who drafted suitable replies or just wrote NO or YES across the letter. I presume he then left to call on factories or confer with the major.

Before the end of the working day I took the letters to the major for signature. Once those letters were signed, I put them into envelopes and left them to be posted by one of the soldiers. We were then all ready to go home. I had no idea where the others lived, and I cared less. I had a roof over my head, and I had no doubt that the sergeant had found the required accommodation for all his men.

I cannot say that life was more hectic; it was different. I noticed a warm relationship develop between the sergeant and the elderly captain, who had allowed himself at times a little whisky during the day and was none too steady on his feet, but sitting on the pillion behind the sergeant on his motorcycle, he looked as steady as a rock. A meaningful job was found for the captain, because I always saw him busy at his desk. This was not the case with the German ex-army officer. He became increasingly unpopular, finding fault with everyone, and was eventually sidelined in terms of his responsibilities. I believe he finally left of his own free will.

Once everything in the office was running smoothly, the sergeant sometimes relaxed by sitting on a chair at the end of one of our desks. To our surprise he spoke good German and appeared to look for an opportunity to talk to us in German. He told us he had been a French interpreter in North Africa and, coming north through Italy, had started to learn Italian. As for German, he had learnt that before he joined the army. Now was the time to learn more and perfect his skills. His name was Ernest, although we always addressed them all in terms of their rank.

I do not remember any of the military staff having gone home for Christmas, but they all had made friends, British and German, in the Hannover area, where they had worked before joining us in Lüneburg. They were all invited to spend the festive season with those friends. A few days before Christmas they left one by one, and the office became deserted. Ernest had always gone back to Hannover for weekends. He had many friends there while, for the others, it was a less frequent opportunity to escape from work. Eventually, we packed up as well and wished those who were left a happy Christmas too.

It was a very humble Christmas for our family. I remember going to church and enjoying a vegetable stew on Christmas day. We all received surprise gifts, handmade for one another out of an old pullover or a piece of wood, and after a few more days the year 1945 drew to a close. People everywhere were looking forward to the spring. Bit by bit things would improve when the cold winter had passed. At present there was neither adequate food nor fuel for heating.

9.

Early in the New Year, Treptow came into focus again. The province of Pommern, in which Treptow was situated, was at first called a Polish Protectorate. In reality it had become a Polish province. My views on this situation had not altered. These changes were inevitable and understandable. Many Germans had lost their homes in the bombing as indeed had British families, and some of us had our homes confiscated, the price we had paid for having started and lost the war. I bore no ill feeling towards the Poles. The Soviet Union had helped itself to a piece of Poland in the east and, as compensation, handed the Poles a piece of Germany. No-one asked the Poles what they thought about that deal. They, in turn, did not make the mistake of former generations, to wait for the next German uprising. They expelled the residents from their country and told them to walk along the Baltic beaches until they had reached West Germany. That was where they now belonged.

My father received a letter from the Red Cross to say that his mother, his sister and her husband had arrived in Lübeck from the Polish Protectorate. At present they were staying in a very large refugee camp, safely looked after in West Germany, but that could only be regarded as temporary accommodation. Could he, my father, put them up? If not, could he at least provide for his mother?

Apart from the fact that our landlady would not have tolerated those changes in our circumstances, with three generations to a room and my sister and I sharing a bed, we had to decline the offer. Things would have been different, if taking in relatives had been a matter of life and death. As it was, my relatives would eventually be allocated alternative accommodation and in any case, my grandmother had another daughter living in comfortable circumstances in Wiesbaden. We were sure that something could be sorted out to everyone's satisfaction.

My father answered the letter with a heavy heart because, until a solution would be found, my grandmother had only a single blanket on the bare ground inside a tent and a daily meal from a soup kitchen. I think she had recently turned eighty.

I do not know why I mentioned that in the office, but a few days later the sergeant, Ernest, took me to one side and wondered if it would not be possible to take some things to the refugee camp, to make life more comfortable for my grandmother. "Perhaps some chairs, a couple of blankets and some extra food," he added. I told him not to worry, but he kept on turning that possibility over in his mind, until he had found a solution.

"I can take the Bedford," he said. "I can also lay my hands on three wicker-work chairs, three blankets and some food. Would that help?"

"Of course, it would." I was almost in tears. "But who's going to drive the Bedford, Sergeant?"

"I'll drive it, if you come with me. You know the old lady! 'I don't."

I was delighted and I agreed. We set off at dusk. By the time we reached the *Autobahn* it was dark. To be on that motorway in these days is a hair-raising experience, but in those days there was only a petrol allowance for essential services. Besides, ninety per cent of the traffic consisted of military vehicles and even those were not as much in evidence at night. Now and then, just for a second in the course of our conversations, our eyes met in the dim light of the instrument panel on the dashboard. There was not much he could see as I found out when I glanced sideways at him. I had all the time in the world to do so because I was not driving, and yet I dreaded our eyes meeting and giving away any interest I might have for the man sitting beside me. Being together for so long, not occupied with office work, was a new experience for us. I found myself musing - a man in British army uniform and a girl who only a year ago had worn the swastika on her Labour Service uniform and then on her Red Cross uniform; did that make sense? I know I had had no choice in the matter, certainly the labour service was forced on me and as I was told at *Munsterlager,* my nursing should not have been affiliated to the Nazi party. However, even if one made allowances and found excuses for all the swastikas that had littered my shoe box; were the occupants of this lorry not an odd combination? "Not at all," I told myself, and I thought of a hundred reasons why we were not. We both could speak English and German, we both could type and telephone, we both liked trifle and ice cream and *Bratkartoffeln* (potatoes first boiled and then fried). Those were enough reasons for us to be happy together. I thought of other things we might enjoy together, but I'll not mention those here.

"Please talk to me," he said, "or I'm going to fall asleep." Excuse me, but that was a little white lie! We were neither of us tired. We were wide awake, and very aware of each other; maybe both waiting for a little encouragement which never materialised. In any case, what could we do, driving in the dark with an army lorry wrapped round us? He obviously wanted to hear more about me and I wanted to learn more about him and so we started talking. He had not been home for five years. He must have forgotten what England was like. He certainly had had no opportunity to meet girls in his own country. The war was to blame, no-one else. The war dominated our conversation. He told me how he had been wounded in Italy, his journey north to Germany and he always mentioned his beloved motorbike. He was looking forward to going home now.

We arrived at the refugee camp in the middle of the night and found the Red Cross staff on duty. They were helpful and soon found my family. My grandmother greeted both of us with open arms and my uncle and aunt were also pleased to see us. To be able to sit in a chair with an extra blanket round her would make such a difference, and all this wonderful food; so much kindness. They would take everything with them when they were relocated, or at least what was left of it. For us, it was soon time to return to Lüneburg and after another round of hugs we took our leave and arrived back at our base in the early hours of the following day.

For Ernest and I nothing had changed in our relationship but I think at that time we both wondered - just a tiny bit - if things might one day change.

He sometimes surprised me with his sudden ideas. They seemed to come into his head for no reason at all, like the next question. "Would you like to learn to drive?" he asked one day when spring was on its way and the days were getting longer. The roads through the heath-land were ideal to get acquainted with a stubborn gearbox, particularly when the vehicle involved was a five-ton Bedford.

He always preferred driving to walking, because his feet refused to take part in longer hikes, but he was always good company. He never made promises, unless he knew he would be able to keep them. We just seemed to drift along nicely - carefree. I know I thought a lot about him in those days, trying to imagine what course events might take and whether a longer-term relationship was an option. I had commitments at home; so had he. Those would be very hard to satisfy. We both concentrated on our present happiness and lived for the moment. We were attracted to each other, but we were certainly not in love.

We had a lot in common, having both been brought up in a city, he in London and I in Berlin. We were both fond of the countryside. Somehow, we only counted what we had in common. All the things in which we differed were either never noticed at that time or they were noticed and not mentioned. More likely, we felt that little things of disagreement could so easily be ironed out.

The heather around us had long since finished blooming. Now it was the turn of the birches to burst into bud and add that lovely lime green to the landscape. I had made friends with an operator of a cinema projector. She was older than I was and had a piano. That must have been the attraction. Her son, in his early teens, was one of those gifted pianists who never had a lesson in his life, and yet could sit at the piano and play all the current pop songs with some sort of pleasing accompaniment. I called at their flat sometimes, but I was too embarrassed to invite them into our room in the attic. They had always lived in Lüneburg and had lost nothing. The friendship was doomed from the start.

I was more likely to lose myself on one of the nature trails around the town, and I was happy there. The one thing I would have given the world to own was a bicycle, but I did not possess anything which would have been in demand and which I could have exchanged for a bicycle on the black market. I had to content myself with enviously staring at bicycles which other people rode. Occasionally, maybe once a week, Ernest and I arranged to meet in the evening for a brief driving lesson. He seemed to be more settled now. He had given up riding his motorcycle to Hannover every weekend. Some of his friends came to Lüneburg instead. We both knew that one day he would go home to his mother.

At my home we had to get used to the idea that my father would be out of work again. The unit for which he worked was being disbanded and the British staff repatriated. There were a couple of weeks to go before that would take place, but my father started looking for work as soon as he was told about the closure. Industry had not yet recovered sufficiently to make it possible for people of my father's age and ability to find work. He tried repeatedly to secure a job, but never with success.

My mother and I still worked in the laundry business, but there was not enough room for my father to participate. We bought little luxuries for the cigarettes we earned. Most of those luxuries were really necessities. At that rate, it would have taken me twenty years to save up for a bicycle.

It would also not be long now before the work in our office would be taken over by the military government. The British soldiers, responsible up to then for the allocation of building materials, would also be sent home. They joked when they explained that 'pen-pushers' would soon take over the running of the office. They were too elated to care. Ernest and I viewed the situation rather differently.

I don't know whose idea it was, but one day it was arranged that 'the sergeant' should meet my parents and Eka. I had thought that it would be prudent to inform the landlady, in case she thought British troops were about to requisition her house. Her reaction was completely unexpected. She was embarrassed at the thought of a stranger seeing the shabby way in which she had treated the refugees. To keep her happy, we reluctantly agreed to use her drawing room. The family silver was laid out, but I drew the line at using her bone china cups. To break one of those would have broken my heart. A couple of our Berlin plates and mugs were all we needed for what we could provide. I remember on offer were pieces of dry bread with soft cheese and pieces of dry bread decorated with chocolate chips and nuts from a bar of chocolate which Ernest had brought and there was plenty of fruit. We really wanted just a cup of tea, but somehow it looked better if a plate with something stood in the middle of the table. Neither my mother nor my father could speak English. I, therefore, welcomed the fact that Ernest could speak

German, but no-one felt relaxed and I was pleased when the stilted conversation came to an end. I carried the crockery up to our room and, after I returned, Ernest got up to leave.

A few days later he was promoted to staff sergeant. I remember being surprised that this honour was all he received. He could quite easily have run the whole project single-handedly. I learned then that he was offered a commission, but had refused to accept it. "Do you not want to be an officer, sergeant?" I had asked. He must have had his reasons. He shook his head and all he said was: "How about you calling me Ernest? That would be something to celebrate!" The switch of subject came as a complete surprise although, maybe, it should not have done. I agreed, but not inside the office.

I had been so preoccupied with my own family that I had overlooked Ernest's situation as regards his mother. Should he tell her in his letters that he had a German girlfriend? When would be the best time to tell her? Were his feelings towards me serious enough to tell her at all? He had never even told me that he enjoyed my company! He certainly had never behaved as though he was in love with me. I spent my time trying to read meaning into what he said and the things he did. Perhaps we were just good friends.

All that changed one day when he gave me his mother's letter to read, the first of many. Those letters arrived about once a fortnight. They were short, always expressing her love for her only child. There were a few sentences about her work, the food she could buy, the weather and maybe what work would have to be done to the house. Not having seen her son for five years made it difficult for her to find anything else to write about. Nothing exciting ever seemed to happen to her. She lived in a peaceful world in Wiltshire where the return of her son was really all she could think and dream about.

Why had Ernest given me those letters to read? Was it to tell me how the English people lived? Suddenly a reference to me appeared in her letters. He must have told her about me. "Of course she can come and she'll be very welcome," she wrote, assuming that I would come for a holiday. Ernest's mother was not to know that the invitation was meaningless, because German nationals could not travel to England for a holiday at that time. I never knew what Ernest wrote to her, but in her next letter, which was a little delayed, she wrote, "Let me know in good time when she is coming and whether you can come with her."

There were days when Ernest was away visiting factories, when we never saw each other. Sporadically the driving lessons in the heathland continued, but they were short and to the point because Ernest was expected somewhere else. I was now convinced that Ernest and I where indeed just good friends.

Overshadowing our relationship was the knowledge that Ernest would go back to England in the foreseeable future. Indeed, moving on was part of the plan for our family too. A relative in Wiesbaden, in the American zone of occupation, had written to say she could put us up. Her husband had fallen at Stalingrad, and there was plenty of room in the flat. The rent could be shared, so that each family would benefit. It sounded ideal. Maybe my father could find work there. I certainly could, and so might my mother. Poor Eka had to change school again, but she was well used to that now.

Our room under the rafters was so inconvenient at times. We would have to find somewhere better. We knew from experience that living with relatives can be very trying, but we told ourselves that it does not have to be like that. We would, of course, never be free and independent, unless we had our own little flat. That idea was still a far-off dream. The huge building programme in Germany was lagging behind. It was expensive to rent a self-contained apartment. It seemed you either had one of those before the war and it had suffered no damage, or you made do with a room in someone else's flat. Sadly, it would take a few more moves before my parents had their first one-bedroom flat. One thing we could rely on; Wiesbaden was a beautiful town. Hardly anything had been destroyed. The surrounding countryside was the envy of many people. It was fruit growing land. We thought we would love it there, at least my parents thought so.

My friendship with Ernest had nothing to do with my parents wanting to move away from Lüneburg. It would have been understandable. We were a very close-knit family, and they might have feared that I would be irretrievably unhappy in another country, any other country. I must, however, say they had my happiness at heart, not theirs'. They often reiterated that I had done so much for them, that they would never stand in the way of my wishes regarding my future.

In those days regulations stipulated that it would take twelve months from making the application to obtaining a visa for entry to the United Kingdom. Even the British government must have felt it prudent to introduce a 'cooling off time' for 'mixed marriages'.

The time passed very quickly. I handed in my notice. Ernest wrote a 'To whom it may concern' reference for me in glowing colours. Was I really that good? I doubt it! I left him my new address in Wiesbaden. It was over 400 kilometres south of us. We promised to write to each other and he said that he would try and visit us. I knew he meant what he said, but I had some doubts at that time about such a long drive.

My father gave in his notice, Eka was taken out of school, the last laundry parcels were delivered and we were ready to go. We owned little more than we did when we left Berlin. The journey south to Wiesbaden would be very different though to our last one – from Berlin. Passenger trains had been re-introduced. We would travel in comfort this time and it would all be within West Germany.

Early summer in that part of Germany was a taste of the baking heat that was to come, but we were convinced, we would get used to the different climate. The reception on our arrival was extremely friendly. We rented a room in my cousin's flat. It had three beds, a couch and a large sofa, so that Eka and I could now sleep separately. My cousin kept two rooms, one for herself and one for her two small children. Kitchen facilities were shared, as was the bathroom. All told, conditions were a great improvement on what we had been used to in Lüneburg.

My mother took Eka to the nearest grammar school. The form teacher put her on a seat at the back of the class, and there she stayed, until it was time for her to toddle back to her new home - alone. She did not make many friends in Wiesbaden, but I remember one girl she particularly liked. They were often seen together, doing homework or playing. She adjusted to her new environment. It was expected of her.

Armed with my reference, I went to an American unit looking for an experienced typist/interpreter. Already at the brief interview I was given the nickname 'Limey Girl.' I understand it is a slang name given by an American to an English girl, dating back to the times when English sailors received rations of lime juice or fruit on long voyages as vitamin supplements. My accent, when speaking English, was indeed very different from that spoken by my superiors and there Miss Understood entered my mind again. What must that American girl in our class have sounded like to Miss Understood? I can still hear her lecturing us about the purity of the King's English. In my present situation I think she would have preferred to have the ground swallow her up rather than converse with the people from across the Atlantic.

One of the lady officers once remarked that I must have had a good teacher to be so 'nicely spoken'.

"Maybe, Madam," I answered. "My teacher certainly had a lot to say about your country and the American people."

"Bless her. Was she English herself?" I nodded. The officer continued, "You see, the Americans and the British have so much in common that they would do anything for one another. Don't you think?"

"I don't know and it doesn't matter what I think," I answered. "My teacher certainly would have agreed with you," I lied; and would have told any number of lies for Miss Understood.

Unfortunately my father could only find casual work, and my mother was precluded from going out to work at all, because she was expected to look after my cousin's small children. This aspect of us moving to Wiesbaden had never been discussed. Like the small print on a contract we were not aware of that clause in our rent agreement. Little was said, but the money which we needed for rations and rent was just not enough, although on the market it was almost worthless.

We enjoyed the countryside, and the town itself certainly lived up to its expectations, but neither was of great benefit to us if my mother was precluded from going out to work. As time went on, I was the only bread-winner in the family. We struggled on. The highlights of our stay in Wiesbaden were Ernest's visits. He braved the drive from Lüneburg every weekend with very few exceptions. We could only offer him a bed on the sofa but that was not a problem to him. In that delightful surrounding of hills, woods and orchards - The Taunus - we really enjoyed the time we could spend together. Hand in hand we explored all the beauty trails, but time was always short. We were either expected back for a meal or we made preparations for his drive back to Lüneburg. On one occasion he asked my father formally if he could marry me if all went well, but he was honest enough to point out that as yet he had no home, no job and no date to offer me.

As the weeks went by we drew ever nearer to the date when Ernest would be repatriated and go home to Wiltshire, where his mother now lived in a rented house on her own. Once he had gone, shortage of money and space made us, once again, consider moving somewhere else. Our few possessions were easily collected and packed, but where would we go? I used a week's leave to do some exploring. I was anxious to find work for my father or my mother, so that their lives were secure, before I left for England. I also wanted to find better accommodation for them. I knew no other town in West Germany as well as Lüneburg and so I bought a ticket back there. It was a long journey on which I had plenty of time to evaluate my options. I was sure that, if I had wanted, I would have had no problem in securing my old job again with the Royal Engineers, but it wasn't a job for me that was at issue here. I spent two days walking the streets, scanning the job centre and calling at factories which might have vacancies now or in the future, but all to no avail.

Out of nostalgia I walked to the outskirts of the town, to my previous place of work. The Royal Engineers had gone. I was sure they had not left the country. So I enquired next door what had happened to the unit. They had moved to Braunschweig (Brunswick), a bigger town, also quite near the border with East Germany. Suddenly I wondered if they would have a job for my father. He was not a handyman and that was his downfall, but he would have a go at anything which presented itself. He had found a job with the occupation forces once before, why should he not try again? If the major, who was in charge of the office in which I had been employed, needed an odd-job-man, he would certainly consider my father for that vacancy. I bought a ticket to Braunschweig.

British units usually kept together in one part of a town. I only had to ask where that part was in Braunschweig. When I found their base, I was amazed at how large it had become. Gone were the days of semi-detached private houses; I now stood in front of a building the size of a *Rathaus*. Steps, three metres wide, led up to the front door of what looked more like the council offices of a medium-sized town than a small procurement office.

I let myself in and was immediately greeted like a long-lost friend. I passed many new faces as well. In all respects the enterprise had grown beyond recognition. A cup of coffee was waiting for me in the kitchen and, while drinking it, a hundred questions were fired at me. Everyone assumed that I had come to see how they were doing, that I had travelled over 400 kilometres to do just that. I did not enlighten them because my business was with the major and not with the rest of the staff, German or British.

Eventually I extricated myself from the crowd and knocked at the door of the major's office. I would have known his brisk voice anywhere when he called me in. As usual his room was wreathed with cigarette smoke, but through it I saw his face, split in half by a huge grin. "Have they not arrested you yet?" he burst out as he left his chair and came towards me, his hand outstretched.

"Not yet, Sir, they haven't got enough evidence yet. They need your testimony to bring charges."

"Is that so? They'll get nothing out of me," he answered, still grinning.

"No, well, I suppose the bit of bartering worked both ways," I stammered.

"You mean if I drop you in it, you'll do the same for me?" His grin was almost hidden but a twinkle in his eye gave him away. He made it sound as though we had robbed a bank together.

"You know me better than that, Sir," I joked.

"Anyway, you didn't come here to sell eggs! What brought you here? Come on, out with it! There's nothing I would be interested in buying, I'm sure."

He knew from our days in Lüneburg that Ernest and I planned to marry. I think he also looked the other way when Ernest needed transport to go to Wiesbaden. We had been like one big happy family in those days. When I explained, he could well understand my concern to see my parents settled before leaving them. On the other hand, he knew that he would one day have to hand over the office to Military Government. They might cut down on staff; they might move somewhere different again. He could only help me in the short term.

"That's all I'm asking," I said. "My father will soon get a small pension. With a little extra my mother could earn, they would manage. It's the immediate future I'm worried about."

Sitting at opposite sides of his desk, we worked out a plan. A house had been requisitioned for the major. He wanted to employ someone to operate the coal-fired boiler, part time. If my mother would cook for him and sometimes for his guests, he would employ her in the afternoon and early evening. If they agreed to that, he could supply them with a small dwelling consisting of several rooms. Although pre-fabricated, it was well built and included a little iron stove. That all amounted to one full-time job divided between my parents. I could have hugged him.

He drew a map to show me the layout. My parents' home would be located at the end of an unmade road. Opposite stood a private house occupied by a fellow British major – Major Lewis. The promise was that the key to what could be my parents' home would be left with Major Lewis. I could collect the key from there, move in and then bring my parents to see him here in the office when they were ready to start work. It could not be too soon. For my part, I promised that I would return as soon as I could.

So much had depended on the outcome of my journey here that I now felt almost an anticlimax after all the worry of the past. We would have our own front-door key. We would live in a residential area with the countryside beside us. We would be in Heaven - and rent-free! Bless this Scotsman with his immaculate moustache. I was standing up to leave when he stopped me. "What I really need now is a typist/interpreter," he said.

I was beside myself with joy. "Do you? Well here I am!" I cried, wiping away a tear.

I walked back to the station, my mission accomplished. I could have run to catch the next train, but I decided to wait for the following one because I felt I had deserved a little treat. Sitting on a bench at the station, I counted my money. First I bought my ticket and then I dived into the station restaurant and ordered a plate of fried potatoes and two eggs. I had not eaten so well for a long time. Instead of savouring the meal, though, I ate hurriedly. I took the major's sketch from my pocket and decided to take a quick walk to see the area myself. It was a long walk but, without the burden of luggage, I set off in high spirits. I was pleasantly surprised when I looked around the outside of what would be my parent's next home. It was well-built in heavy timber and so constructed that there was a space underneath the building where one could comfortably bed down.

In fact this space already served that purpose. A dachshund crawled out from underneath and we made friends there and then. He wore a leather collar with his name. It was Napoleon. In the restaurant I had wrapped a few fried potatoes in a serviette for my tea. When I offered these to Napoleon our friendship was sealed for eternity. I figured his need was greater than mine. Besides, I knew I still had enough money left to buy a roll to take on the journey.

Napoleon had dug himself a bed under the house and, from that position of seclusion, could view a potential battle-ground and a potential enemy from a safe distance. My appearance had obviously triggered a hope of mutual interest in him. Not only did he see me as a source of food, he would also benefit from an ally in any battle to come. Judging by the two scars on his back, he had amassed some relevant experience.

I could now explain to my parents what to expect if they moved to Braunschweig. I looked across to the house opposite where I was to collect the key. Two English speaking children played in the garden. It was one of the British married family houses. After saying good-bye to Napoleon I walked back to the station, caught the next train, and arrived in Wiesbaden in the early hours of the following morning. I had much to tell my parents. They were delighted and could hardly wait for the day of our departure. There was plenty still to be arranged, but that would go smoothly with such pleasant prospects in view.

As a first step towards moving, I handed in my notice. We all had to call at the police station to inform them about our intended departure and Eka had to be taken out of her school – once again.

In a way, living in Wiesbaden had been a trying time for us. My father had been out of work and my mother was tied to baby-sitting. There had been a shortage of money and no hope for the future which had caused friction within the family. I first noticed this when my father wanted to look after his mother. He had felt a complete failure, not being able to provide for her. As long as my grandmother had daughters who could care for her, my mother refused to accommodate her in our one and only room. Besides, my cousin with whom we shared the flat would not have agreed to that arrangement. There were much more suitable options. Not until my grandmother moved to one of her daughters did harmony return to our family.

On the day before we left I collected my final pay-packet. My mother accompanied Eka to school and arranged for her name to be taken off the register. They walked home together, Eka almost in tears.

10.

When we arrived at our new home in Braunschweig, we could hardly believe our good luck. The place had been furnished before we arrived. There were two homely bedrooms with two beds in each of them. Mattresses had been provided, but no bed-linen. In the living room stood a heating stove and a cooking stove with a sink and water tap beside it. It was a spacious room with a table and four chairs in the centre and there was a toilet, wash-hand basin and some kind of shower through a door on the right. Even then, we were only occupying half the building. Napoleon, who lived underneath, was responsible for security! He took his duties very seriously, for he would not even come inside when invited. Any food intended for him had to be placed onto the lower of six wide steps which led to the front door.

The family opposite us, Major and Mrs. Lewis, were rarely in. Up to now they had been the provider of Napoleon's food, but that had been so irregular that we came to an agreement about sharing responsibility for feeding the dog. Before they went away they would leave a bag of scraps with us and, by adding some food, we would divide it into daily portions and leave the appropriate ration on the door step.

I had met Major and Mrs. Lewis first when I collected the key. They were friendly but withdrawn. Eventually they returned to the United Kingdom and the German owner moved back into his house. That did not happen until after I had gone to England. The English couple sometimes sought my help as interpreter when they wanted to remonstrate with a tradesman or when leaflets had been posted which they did not understand. On those occasions they showed gratitude and invariably handed me a bar of chocolate.

Napoleon soon got the message that we were now in charge of feeding him. If for some reason we were late, he would sit on the doorstep and let out yelps at ten second intervals. Apart from that he was a very quiet dog unless his territory was threatened. Dog owners, taking their pets for a walk along our road and to the edge of the field beyond, would respectfully keep their charges on the lead when passing. Napoleon's two big eyes were always glued to the bottom beam of the hut, just in case some roaming, care-free mongrel decided to investigate his command post this side of the East/West border. In that event Napoleon would charge out and take on the intruder until he was either defeated or had fled back to the Soviets. Borders were sacred now, to the British, to the Germans... and apparently to all Western dogs.

To me Napoleon's most remarkable attribute was his loyalty. No amount of persuasion would have enticed him to stay behind when I set off to work in the morning. I had to walk briskly which he could not do with his short legs. The outcome was that I arrived first at work and by eleven o'clock he sat on the office steps waiting for his biscuit. Having once walked that distance with me when there was plenty of time, he had remembered every turning and road crossing which had to be negotiated. I have no idea what else he had been given to eat when I was not looking, for he was a great favourite with all the soldiers, but, as with our home, he would not enter the building.

When it was time for me to go home in the evening, the same happened in reverse. The only difference being, that I would walk slower to give us a chance to stay together. However short his legs may have been, they still functioned like clockwork.

There were now eight German employees in the office. I was the only woman. The men had all belonged to the German forces and had been released from prisoner of war camps. They could all speak reasonable English, in any case enough to make themselves understood. Most of them acted as mediators between firms and our procurement office, either by telephone or on foot in case visual checks were required. They were well aware of the fact that the office was run by former enemies, but also that its objective was to improve the German economy. For that reason ex-soldiers and officers of all ideologies had joined forces for the common good. I was probably best placed to judge whether the denazification process of individuals had been successful. It was difficult to tell.

My judgement in that respect was only of interest to myself. I had no illusions that all Nazis had disappeared overnight. The three or four men, who still clung to the old values, had to learn the benefits of democracy. They had to digest or choke on pictures of the Hitler regime and, as long as those people kept their views to themselves, they did no harm. Having shouted *Heil Hitler* all their lives, they needed time to adjust. They had been cleared of having committed war crimes and that was good enough for the British.

I am not sure what prompted the idea of providing a hot midday stew for the German staff, but there were good reasons. Some men who had escaped from Soviet captivity were so thin that they were really unfit for work, some still lived rough and some had not yet come to terms with regular food and so could not plan their rations wisely. They would eat everything in two days and then starve for three. For many that had been a reality for years. I am sure the soup (or stew) kitchen had nothing to do with 'winning hearts and minds'. That came later.

The major spoke to me about food for the German employees and I then discussed this with my mother. A day later two large tables and ten chairs were delivered to our home. Two large cooking pots, a sack of coal, a sack of potatoes and a large box of corned beef arrived with the same delivery. A day later baked beans and cabbages were added to our store. My mother became a full-time employee, working mornings at home and afternoons and early evenings in the major's house. Not only the staff of our office, but our whole family was suddenly provided with a daily hot meal and my mother managed to serve this in such appetising variety that it became the highlight of every working day.

The five-ton Bedford provided the transport to our home and back and, to my surprise, even Napoleon accepted a lift both ways, although I did discover later that this was another ploy to obtain food. Returning to the office after his meal, Napoleon resumed sunning himself on the steps. It all worked very smoothly for a few weeks, and then this generous gesture by the British came to an abrupt end. The major noticed that the Bedford used too much petrol, even taking the added mileage into account. He had a twenty-four hour watch put on the vehicle and soon discovered that one of the German employees was regularly siphoning petrol out of the tank at night.

It was a former Luftwaffe pilot who was summoned to the major's office. At first he vehemently denied any knowledge, but when an abundance of witnesses to the crime were produced, he eventually pleaded guilty. "Thanks to you," said the major, "there'll be no more meals served to your fellow Germans and as from today you're relieved of your job in this office."

I had to write the letter informing the labour exchange of the pilot's dismissal. Finding other employment of even the most menial kind would have been very difficult for the former pilot. The pieces of furniture which had been brought to our home for this catering were now redundant, but they were left in place, a permanent reminder of someone's greed. The culprit had no car. He had stolen the petrol to be sold on the black market. Now his fellow Germans were very angry with him. I heard at a later date that he had left the town because he no longer felt safe living there.

The major, of all people, had nothing against the black market, but he despised the stealing. The black market, he explained to me, was a place for buying and selling; buying what you could afford and selling what you owned. It was not the pilot's right to sell what did not belong to him. The major had made his point and dropped the subject. He had trusted me on many occasions to buy things for him on the black market, but that was different. He used to tell me what he would like to buy and I made enquiries and maybe brought a piece of jewellery to let him see it. I worked on a set amount of commission in the form of cigarettes. Since our laundry had closed down, I needed another source of 'hard currency', cigarettes and coffee being the only commodities of value. I needed a blanket, a pair of shoes and I fancied a few yards of skirt material. None of that could have been bought in a shop. It was all there though - somewhere - hidden in cellars and lofts, buried in straw or sand-pits. When in 1948 the new currency was finally issued, and you could exchange just forty Reichmarks for forty Deutsch marks, the shops were full of goods. The people just stood and stared, but had to earn first in order to buy. I lived in England at that time and could only imagine what life was like in Germany.

Back in Braunschweig we had to make do without our midday meal. I could not have walked the distance to and from work twice a day, but we were all earning something and could cover such expenses as heat, light and the food available on our ration cards. Harmony had returned to our family and we made the most of our time together. There were still several months to go before I would leave for England.

The British military government, it was rumoured, would shortly take over our procurement office, which probably meant that the major and all his engineers would be allowed to return home. I asked the major if there was any truth in that rumour, since they had talked about it so often. He genuinely did not know. When it happened, it would do so with little warning.

Quite likely at that time our home would also be returned to its rightful owner. We did not have to move out in a hurry, but it would be prudent to investigate the housing market. The major assured me that he would give my parents a very good testimony, if he were to leave, so that they would easily find work elsewhere. He could do no more.

There was always a silver lining to our predicaments. One Sunday, when out for a walk, we saw a notice in a shop window, advertising two rooms and the use of the kitchen. A middle-aged lady lived there, mostly on her own, because her husband was a long distance train driver. We went to have a look at the house, four stories high and very old, but to us it seemed structurally sound. After all, we had no intention of buying it. We walked in and climbed the stairs. The toilets were situated half way between the floors, one for every three flats. The flats themselves were sublet. This was the kind of property which should long since have been demolished, but was kept standing until some of the bomb-damaged buildings had been replaced. Above all, the rent would be cheap. The lady tenant was probably looking for company.

We walked home and talked about what we had seen. We considered the proximity to all the services and shops. Some of the nearby factories would surely employ one of my parents after I had left. Although always the youngest in her class, Eka was doing well at school and we were delighted for her. She would do even better once we lived nearer to her school and to the city centre. These considerations are important when you have no car.

The following Saturday we called on the lady who was currently occupying the flat. Both my mother and I knew immediately that we would get on well with her. She was very slight and her kind face was marked with deep wrinkles, although she could only have been in her forties. We felt that she must have had a hard life to look back on. She expected nothing from us except a modest, regular rent, and offered to let two rooms either furnished or unfurnished. In the case of the latter option the rent would be further reduced. She pleaded with us to be patient for a month as regards the move, because she would be away from home for that time. This arrangement suited us well, as we were in no immediate hurry to move. We just wanted to make plans for the future.

Another joyous occasion for us was the introduction of a small pension for all past civil servants. My parents could not have lived on that pension, but it was a great help and there were already plans drawn up for future increases, depending on the economic state of the country as a whole.

As the time of my departure drew nearer, I had to undergo several examinations by a German and by a British doctor, and I had to be vaccinated against numerous diseases. When diphtheria was mentioned, I explained to the doctor that I had been a carrier. I don't think he was quite sure whether to give me the required injection or not. In the end he felt it could do no harm and went ahead. However, the newly injected fluid stayed in an ever growing lump in my arm which started to swell up to twice its size. It was extremely painful and eventually had to be lanced to let the vaccine out again.

Other preparations included a mandatory letter of consent to my marriage from my father, because I was under twenty-one, and a note from a minister of religion to the effect that I was, to his knowledge, of good character.

A pleasant surprise awaited us one day. A relative in Berlin wrote to say that he could send on some of our furniture. The only saleable item would be my piano, and the sale of that would pay for the carriage. The items in question were my parents' bedroom suite and several items from the lounge. Since our flat in Berlin had to be cleared, it seemed an ideal solution to be re-united with some of our furniture. My own views or preferences regarding furniture were no longer important, but I was pleased for my parents who would now be able to rent the two rooms unfurnished. That happened as soon as our furniture arrived from Berlin.

One problem remained - Napoleon. What should we do with him? We could not take him with us, and Major and Mrs. Lewis did not want the responsibility of having to feed him. Their time in the occupation forces was also coming to an end. I decided to speak to some of the soldiers at work. I knew they were all fond of Napoleon and I hoped that one would be interested in having Napoleon. This initiative, however, created another problem. There were six prospective 'adopters'. In the end, the six names were written on pieces of paper. Each was used to wrap up a small piece of meat. One of the soldiers generously offered his beret which he put upside down in the middle of the floor and the six little 'parcels' were thrown in. All Napoleon had to do was pick out the name of his new master. That seemed the fairest way of dealing with the situation. He did not want to come in, he had to be carried.

Great excitement followed Napoleon's antics. First, the little 'parcels' were thrown out of the beret and kicked about the room before he chewed away at one piece of paper to get at the meat inside. In one mouthful he devoured it - meat and paper! The soldiers scrambled to recover the remaining 'parcels' to establish by elimination who would be Napoleon's new owner. I was sorry to leave those colleagues with whom such simple situations could spark off so much fun. Times would change of course; we would grow up and stop acting like children.

A few hours after this event, Napoleon's new owner gave me a pack of a hundred cigarettes. "We've all clubbed together because we felt Napoleon was worth it," he declared. I chose not to believe him. More likely they wanted to give me a leaving present which was of little value to them but would mean the world to me. I thanked them and saw the dog installed in the cook's quarters, at least at night. In the day-time he explored Braunschweig. I heard since that, amongst other places, he was seen under our old home, in the five-ton Bedford, on the road to the border and on the train to Hannover. A photograph supported that sighting, his two scars clearly visible. Some creatures are born travellers.

We moved to the centre of Braunschweig as soon as our furniture arrived and, although we shared the flat with a relative stranger, it became the happiest place we had lived in since Berlin. In time, there was more happiness to come for Eka. Her dream had always been to become an actress. Now we lived in the vicinity of a private drama school, she was enrolled there and excelled at both school and drama. One examination after another was passed with flying colours, which convinced my parents that they had finally made the right decision.

Had I made the right decision? The yard-stick with which prospective suitors were measured in those days was their potential ability to survive hard times. Naturally, physical attraction was important, but people who had only one gift were often considered failures. The man who could repair his own shoes and work as a diver if the Russians needed one, even though he was a baker by trade, was sure to find a partner. He was also never out of work. I believe that attribute was something Ernest and I shared and was certainly part of the attraction we had for one another. In settled times such attributes may lose their importance... but it is always useful to have a handy man about the house - and a handy woman.

When it was time for me to leave Germany, our elderly captain took me to the station in his car and handed me a bunch of carnations as a parting present. He was not a man of many words and just said that it had been a pleasure to know me, a girl with determination and a sense of humour. Even those words, I felt, had been learned off by heart, but they were certainly sincere, and I really appreciated his sentiments.

He was a family man and a sensitive man. He was also the man who had offered me a worthwhile job when I needed it most. Now I was lost for words. I did not even give him a hug or a peck on the cheek. His kindness had left me speechless, but he saw me wipe away a few tears. "Thank you so much," I stammered at last.

"That's all right," he said, "I think I know what you want to say. So there's no need to upset yourself." Then he squeezed my hands, wished me well and hurried up the steps to fetch my parents and Eka. I stood there like a lost sheep until they arrived. I knew they would miss me and I would miss them.

As I waited for them I thought how the farewell at the station had such an air of finality about it, and that only my love for Ernest kept me from running away. I was in love, the age-old wish of fulfilment was pulling me one way, whether it was the right one or not. I knew Ernest felt the same way about me, and that made it right.

When they came down the steps to join me Eka had to tell me straight away about her excellent mark in a German essay. I had to be told before 'leaving for ever'.

Then my father talked about all he could think of, so as not to show his emotions. In contrast, my mother just stood as close to me as she could, not saying a word. Those final moments summed up each of their characters so well.

Finally the train steamed into the station. The tears flowed. We clung to each other until I tore myself away, grabbed my case and my carnations and climbed into the first carriage I came to.

Having closed the door, I let down the window. When the train started moving I waved to the receding figures until long after the steam and my tears had obliterated all vision.

It was a through train to the Hook of Holland, but I was not aware of the towns or cities we passed through. I did not notice the passing of the time and it mattered little to me where I was. I was crouched in a corner, the carnations in one hand and a handkerchief in the other. There were a few other German girls in my carriage, the rest of the passengers were military personnel. I prayed and hoped that God would hear me, whether I prayed from Germany or from England. I think He has.

I remember boarding a big ship, in my hand a first class ticket which Ernest had sent me together with a ten pound note, the latter representing two and a half weeks wages. That was a fortune in those days and I almost resented him having paid so much, but it was what he wanted and I would never have criticized his generosity.

The North Sea was pleasantly calm on that late August day. It was light grey in colour reflecting the overcast sky. Presently no more land was in sight and I walked up to the dining room, sinking into the deep carpet. The English upper class moved about here with ease and confidence. I felt conspicuous in my white coat, made out of a blanket. To take it off would have been worse, because the second-hand dress I wore was too short and too tight and yet I felt every bit as proud as all the other passengers. Clothes were only the outer skin of a body, I told myself. That skin could be replaced in seconds - if you had enough money. You could not buy happiness, but you certainly could buy the trimmings. It was up to the individual to make the effort.

I picked a table beside a window, or was it a port hole? Tomorrow morning, I would be able to watch the coast approach and catch the first glimpse of Harwich. Now I was hungry and I ordered a meal. There were plenty of tables waiting to be claimed by passengers. Disregarding that fact, a young lieutenant steered towards me and asked if he could join me. Who was I to say "yes" or "no?" It was his country we were heading for. I nodded. "You're German then," he started the conversation. The coat had obviously given me away. I nodded again.

When our dishes arrived we began to eat in silence, until he could contain himself no longer. "You know, in England we turn the prongs of the fork to face the plate. It prevents you from shovelling the food." At that point I could happily have got up and left the room, but then I thought that perhaps he meant well. After all, those were the little things which I would have to learn and, besides, the food was far too good to leave.

I smiled at him, wiped my mouth with the serviette and said, "I know that in Rome you do as the Romans do, but I did not think we were in Rome yet. I had forgotten that Rome includes the whole of the North Sea as well as all the ships which sail across this sea." I faced him squarely, still smiling.

"Who, may I ask, taught you to speak English," he blurted out.

"Miss Understood."

"I beg your pardon?"

"She owns this ship as much as you do," I said. "She is also English." I turned the fork prongs down and got on with my meal. He certainly did not understand what I was talking about.

Early the following morning I went on deck. The coastline could just be made out, dark grey against light grey. I was getting nervous and excited. Ernest had promised to collect me from Harwich. I had enjoyed the crossing and hoped that there would be more of them. I would visit Germany again, and one day my parents would come to visit us. Sailing along those quiet waters, my future seemed so predictable. Everything would be so easy, almost as though everything had been arranged by God. All I had to do was close my eyes and sail away into the unknown.

When the coastline became clearer, it seemed flat and uninteresting. But then the sun pushed its way through the clouds and added its colours to the landscape and my first impression of England changed completely.

I looked over the side at the waiting crowds. Could I see Ernest? It was difficult with so many faces to choose from. Everyone had come to collect a loved one. I was one of them. I raised myself onto my toes... and there he was. I could see him! I waved my scarf furiously and then he saw me too. Was it just one man waving or two? No, it was only him waving with both arms.

As soon as the ramp to the quayside had been put into place I was the first one to hurry down to terra firma. There I dropped my little case with a few essentials and some useless wedding presents and we were in each others' arms. He pulled me a little to one side to let other people pass. After that we were not interested in who might watch us or whether we were still causing an obstruction. We were blissfully happy and without a care in the world. For us time stood still.

To get away from the crowds we then made our way to the car park and were thankful that all had worked out so well.

"It's a wonder I recognised you, not wearing a uniform," I began. "I'll have to try and get used to that, I suppose."

"Would that be so hard?"

"I don't know."

Silence. There was a painful silence where neither of us knew what to say. Then followed a little cough, before he found the courage to at least whisper. "When were we last on our own, just you and I, when there wasn't someone waiting to see one of us, or depending on us or coming with us?"

"Oh, wait a minute that must have been when we took the old 5-ton Bedford up North. No", I quickly corrected myself, "it was when you wanted to show me the wrecks in the Lüneburg heathland, and that was only an excuse." We both laughed. Then I said: "Of course, in Wiesbaden we were also on our own, but never long enough. We so much enjoyed being together there and I was always looking forward to you coming, but the heathland in Lüneburg we will never forget."

"You can say that again", he now said quite audibly, "I didn't know where else I could propose to you."

"I could have supplied you with a list of venues."

"No, you could not. Someone would have interrupted in some way. I wasn't taking any chances, not with that commitment in mind. I knew what I wanted, but could you have kept serious if someone had knocked at the door or rang the office?" He paused briefly and then continued. "I also have lovely memories of the trip in the 5-ton Bedford to your grandmother. We stopped a couple of times at a lay-by, not to relax, not to switch off mentally, but to switch on. I tried to read your thoughts, only to find that both our heads were full of questions. We were looking for explanations about our private lives and private feelings and whether my desire to be with you sparked off something inside you. In other words; we were looking for similar signs of affection. I would have loved to seduce you there and then, but the thought that someone might imagine I wanted payment for taking some furniture to a refugee camp, prevented me from touching you, not even your little finger. I just wanted to know whether you might one day fall in love with me."

Of course we both remembered the occasion and Ernest went on: "Good job we weren't stopped by the military police. They were always on the look-out for people like us, wasting precious petrol. We could easily have landed in a cell for the night."

He tried to look serious and so did I when I asked: "The same cell?"

"What are you talking about. No such luck. They weren't a marriage council, not the 'Red Caps'."

We had arrived at that huge car which I was convinced was a hire car. It was not. I threw my case on the back seat and we made up for lost time on the front seats.

My mother and my two sisters: Trautchen and Eka.

My piano teacher, Ella.

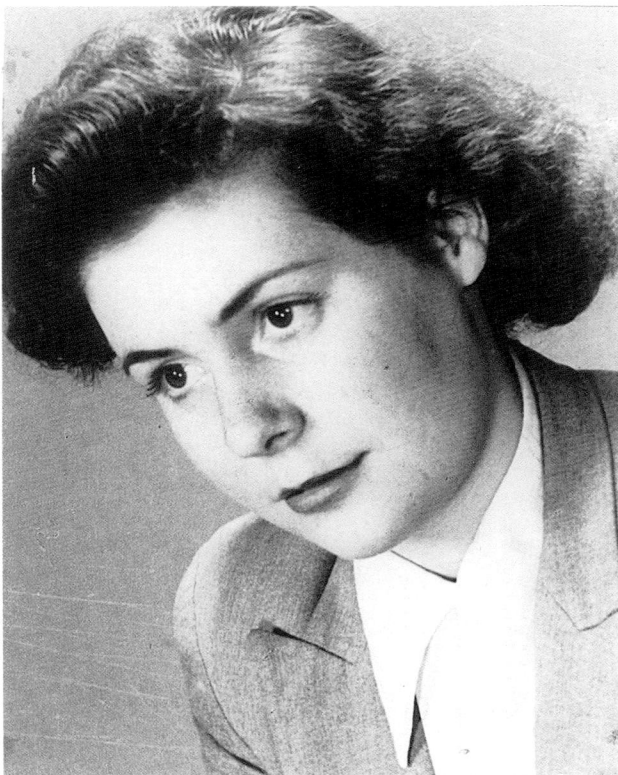

Irene, my travel companion on the long walk to Berlin.

Ernest

My father (68) and I (40)

Eka at the height of her career as actress

Colditz Castle, Saxony, Germany (Oflag IVc). We found no reference to the castle having been a prison of war camp.

Colditz Castle, Oflag IVc, Saxony, Germany, We found a plaque inside the enterance with the following insription which I have translated into English:
In their honour, to our warning
Between 1933 and 1934 this castle served as a security prison.
For many honourable anti-Nazis, this was the start of the road of suffering, to the concentration camps.
They fought so that we may live.

Panzer trench running under the bridge.

Panzer trench which the East German people dug with spade and shovel near the Soviet border in 1944.

Douglas and Ann.

My granddaughter Mair.

My granddaughter Amy.

My grandson Simon and his wife Laura.

The author in her mid-eighties.

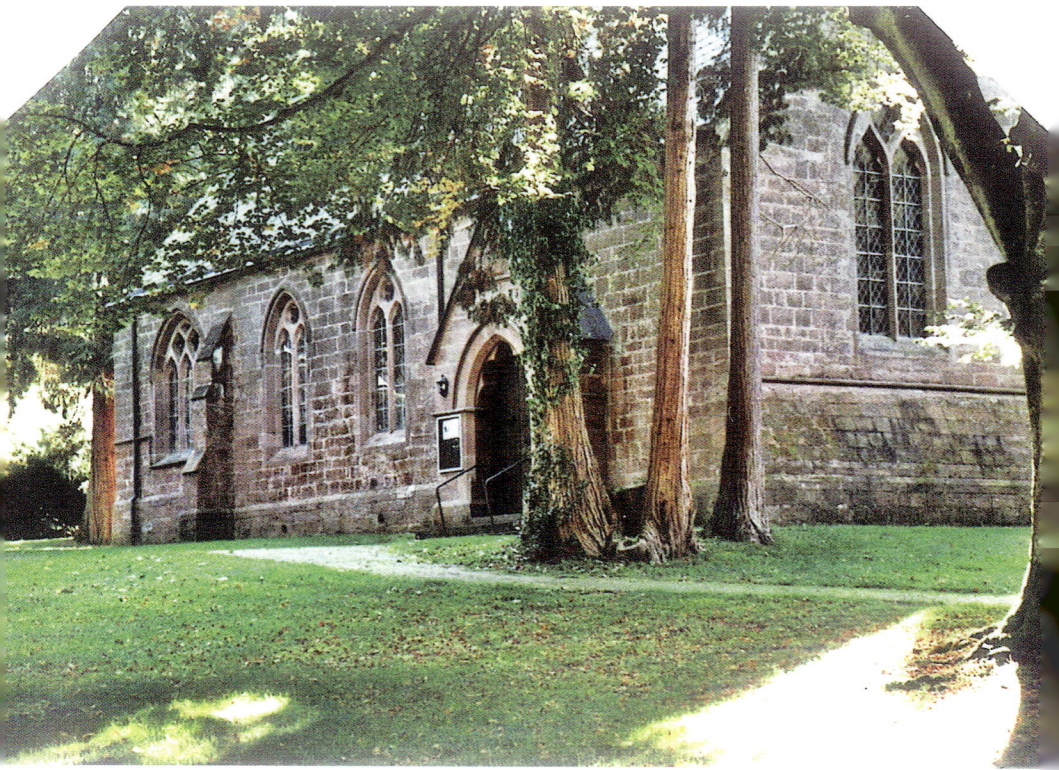

The 'English Church' in Bad Wildbad, Black Forest, Southern Germany ('Bad' translates into 'Spa').

PART TWO

(AN ADULT LOOKS BACK UPON HER PAST)

MEMORIES
OF MY MARRIED LIFE
AND OF PLACES
WHICH I REVISITED

11.

Initially some of my memories had kept me awake at night, but eventually I settled down. I concentrated on the work at hand and enjoyed the novelty of having a husband who loved me as much as I loved him. Between us we would weather any storms and once I had revisited certain places in Poland and Germany I found complete peace of mind, as though I had to make sure that all those things had really happened to me. It was during these revisits that I felt the details and impact of my past much more vividly. Things I had forgotten or which I believed to be unimportant at the time suddenly came to life. Just standing or looking at the various places made me relive the past with the eyes of an adult and the understanding of an adult. I even started to enjoy thinking about my past because I had been so incredibly lucky.

Ernest and I enjoyed a long life together, a long life of common interests, of getting to know each other and finally knowing each other. We had promised to be patient with each other and we were. I lived in a different environment now which was hostile at times, but we weathered such initial storms together, because we loved each other.

To begin with, we settled in Wiltshire and were married there in an Anglican Church. Preparations did not go according to plan. Ernest had belonged to the Methodist Church in London before the war and was also a Sunday school teacher there. His past services at that church were not known in Wiltshire and the Methodist minister refused to marry us. Thankfully, such disappointments were understandable at that time and quite rare.

Preparations for the wedding were very modest. That was common in those days. We did have a honeymoon though. Ernest always maintained that we would not be married without one. I, on the other hand, had never known anyone who would have spent money on a honeymoon, when so much was needed for a new home. Those were the little differences in our make-up.

We each had a bicycle and owned a Morris Oxford, our first car. In it we could accommodate the two bicycles and our luggage. It was huge and seemed extravagant to me, but because of its high petrol consumption, it was cheaper to buy than a small, old car with a very high mileage. At that time we had no intention of travelling long distances in it. We also enjoyed camping, the cheapest mode of having a holiday. In those days it was good enough if you enjoyed the outdoor life.

For Ernest the first few years were also a time of adjustment. He had spent six years in the army, five of them abroad (North Africa, Italy, Belgium and Germany). He was wounded in Italy and was twice in hospital there. When he was finally demobbed he did menial work in England until the right vacancy occurred and then he joined the firm of his choice. He climbed the office ladder to provide a better standard of living for his family. I supported him all the way because I had faith in him. It was against his principals that I should also look for work, unless I enjoyed the work and did not need to supplement the housekeeping. However, the one could not always be separated from the other and we had to accept that I would also contribute to our lifestyle.

Looking back, we had worked hard and we developed a love for boats. Before we met, Ernest had the opportunity to do some sailing in Germany. I was well used to competitive rowing. So you might say, we readily took to water and water became part of our holiday activities at home and later abroad.

Four years after our marriage Ernest was transferred to Northern Ireland, where we seriously hoped to settle down if and when we could find a house to rent. Until such time we made do with one tent inside another, the world's simplest insulated dwelling. It was erected inside a private estate and I believe the firm, for which Ernest worked, had helped with the arrangements. The owner was an elderly widow who made us very welcome and in the end we became good friends. We must have lived at the far end of the estate because when Ernest passed through the entrance gates on his way home from work, he always started whistling, "Onward Christian Soldiers", and that was the time for me to put the potatoes onto the primus stove. In that world of silence his whistle carried a long way, mobile phones had not been invented and it seemed we managed well enough without them. I cannot remember how long we lived in the tents. It was certainly months and not weeks. Eventually we rented our first house in Omagh and built our first twelve foot sailing boat in the lounge of that house. We could only afford a bedroom suite for our furniture coupons. So the lounge was empty anyway and we knew that to get the boat out, the window had to come out as well.

It was also in Omagh that I tried my hand at dressmaking. I had helped my mother a few times to make clothes for my sisters and I could readily pick the style of dress suitable for a given figure, or so I thought. To be on the safe side I took two of my dresses to pieces and then put them together again. I was convinced that nothing could go wrong now. On the strength of that I advertised my imagined skill in the local newspaper and took fright when I received over twenty replies. I admit, initially I made mistakes and had to re-cut an armhole or hem, but after a few months my customers were satisfied first time. After a year I employed a seamstress, for now I had to cope with wedding orders. When that set-up proved to be inadequate, Ernest learned to use the sewing-machine and put in the odd evening or weekend shift. The going rate for an ordinary dress, if the customer brought the material, was one pound and five shillings, for a wedding dress it was five pounds.

As time went by, we invested in cars which were reliable enough to take abroad. There were as yet no roll on and roll off facilities at ports of embarkation. You wasted more time getting on and off a ship in a car and repairing punctures on the road than enjoying the journey. As far as I was concerned, none of our cars was ever loved so much as was my bicycle, a pale blue BSA sports-bike, my wedding present from Ernest. Until I could be persuaded otherwise it remained in our bedroom when not in use. I had wanted a bicycle of my own ever since I was four years old. I could ride a bike all right, but it always belonged to someone else. Ernest had also bought himself a bicycle, this time on hire purchase. His weekly payments amounted roughly to the bus fare which he saved by cycling the ten miles to work. It was the only time we ever bought something without paying for it in full because our funds had dried up and he needed to go to work. We made good use of our bicycles though and I often cycled towards him in the evenings, meeting him half way.

12.

Then, one day, we started our annual visits to my parents, still living in West Germany. I had looked forward to that pleasure for such a long time that, when it happened, it felt like a dream come true. I remember on one such occasion we also drove to Lüneburg. It was a long diversion, but it was, after all, the town where we had first met and worked in the same building for a year. We had now been married for six years and there were no regrets.

We took a right hand turning into the heathland before we reached the town and we both remembered vividly the beautiful countryside with the white sandy, unmade roads winding themselves round large patches of heather and pine. Gone were the burnt out tanks, but our happy memories remained as did the historic facts of Field Marshal Montgomery accepting, as Britain's representative, the unconditional surrender of the German armed forces. Now we parked our car there.

We sat down on a soft heather bed. I slipped off my sandals, buried my feet in the warm sand and started to unpack some tomato sandwiches which I had brought on purpose, while Ernest busied himself with the flask of tea and our plastic cups. Even those simple actions sparked off memories and suddenly we both burst out laughing. "Those tomato sandwiches did it," I shouted. "They were a symbol of our commitment in 1946 to get married one day."

It was now some eight years ago when Ernest stopped me at the office door and whispered: "Fancy coming out to the heathland tomorrow after work? I want to show you some old war-time wrecks and I'll bring some tomato sandwiches and tea."

I tried to look suitably impressed and nodded. A glance through the slightly open door reassured me that Miss Reiter was busy with her typewriter and would not have overheard the words of our arrangement. By the time I turned my head intending to face Ernest again, he had gone. Considering it was our first date which he had arranged, other than driving lessons, it did seem a strange venue since both of us had seen any amount of shot-up and burnt-out war machinery. Let's say, I simply looked forward to being with Ernest privately and having a run out in the countryside. I never expected a special treat.

Ernest was rarely in the office which I shared with Miss Reiter, our only qualified foreign correspondent. Being elderly, she had forgotten most of her English and was not interested in learning anything new. She was an ornament which was allowed to stay because of her qualifications.

Under those circumstances Ernest and I had exchanged certain glances at odd times when he discussed the mail with me. But we never talked about private matters, unless 'the coast was clear'; (for instance on our arrival in the morning when we unintentionally or intentionally ran into each other or when Miss Reiter had to go to the bathroom). These conditions suited the British Army Regulations as well with regard to their non-fraternization orders. At the time, it seemed, every effort was being made to enforce the orders and keep the German women in their places, but 'where there is a will, there is usually also a way'.

Ernest was very friendly with both the captain and the major of the unit. He invariably spent the evening with one of them, discussing problems at work about the distribution of building materials or the integrity of German factory management. He spoke German and French fluently and had visited every factory applying for or receiving aid. Within a large area around Lüneburg he was the liaison between the supervising British control office and the German factories receiving building materials through Marshall-Plan aid. He had refused a commission because he was happier sharing billets with other ranks, but that did not exclude him from being responsible for the day-to-day running of the offices. Some transport was always at hand for him to use, at first only for official runs, but as he made excellent progress in his work, a Volkswagen was made available for his private use in place of his motor cycle. This then was the background to the man who had worked with me in the office and then suddenly asked me out for a run through the Lüneburg Heath (*Lüneburger Heide*).

Sitting now on our heather bed munching our tomato sandwiches, I looked at mine critically and said: "Mind you, on our first private outing you had produced different sandwiches. They were all the same length. The tomatoes were cut as thin as a sheet of paper and put three sixteenths of an inch thick inside the white bread. I had last seen such pure white bread before the war. Then there were egg-cups with pepper and salt which you had fitted with little cardboard lids and a tiny box of chopped onions to sprinkle on the bread if desired. It was all delicious and when you saw how much I enjoyed the 'feast', you turned your head towards me and gave me a kiss on the cheek. I henceforth referred to that delightful experience as 'my tomato kiss with promise'."

"Just a minute," protested Ernest, "you weren't the only one enjoying the tea. Fresh food was like a present from heaven for me too. It could not be bought in a shop, but I had found a source not far from here, tomatoes in a back garden: one pound = two cigarettes. Anyway, I didn't drive to Lüneburg Heath for the sandwiches. I wanted to be with you." He paused briefly while we went on eating and then he continued. "As I remember, one of us suggested having a closer look at these rusty gun-carriers which was probably me. I was always looking for tools. This carry-on resulted in you running away and hiding yourself and before long we played hide and seek among the bushes and the debris."

"I know." I now took up the sequence of events of that day. "Afterwards we clambered onto a burnt out tank. You went inside and when you came out again you proposed to me prancing about on top of the tank and I shouted: 'I will, I will love you and work with you and for you because I enjoy being with you'."

"You stop right there, Madam," Ernest interrupted. "I was not interested in having a maid. I wanted a wife and said so." We both jumped down from the top of the tank. We tumbled over, stood up and knocked the sand off our clothes. Did we love each other enough to last a life time? He took me in his arms and kissed me. We clung together whispering all sorts of sweet promises to one another. We were in dreamland. Ernest was miles from home and I had lost my home. Around us stood the witnesses to our commitments, the silent skeletons of destruction, but the war was over. The cost had been enormous. Future efforts to make peace would have to be enormous too. We were the new generation challenged with implementing the peace. War and peace were man-made, but I thought love just happened to die or to survive and if it survived it would do so for ever. We still clung together and only reluctantly let go. As dusk spread slowly across the heathland we climbed back into the 5-ton Bedford and navigated our way through the maze of scrubland and rusty metal. We knew we would never forget that day.

Next day when I took the letters to the major to be signed I also thanked him. "It was very good of you to let us have the Bedford for the evening, Sir, thank you." He was in his late thirties, bald, but with this magnificent ginger moustache, and when wearing his cap, he looked extremely handsome. He came from Edinburgh. His fiancée, also an officer in the British army, served in another town in Germany. Ernest drove her regularly to Lüneburg at weekends. That was our commanding officer. He acknowledged my thanks with a smile at the same time reading and signing the letters which I had brought. I had no idea how much the major knew about Ernest and me, but I thought quite a lot. He suddenly stopped what he was doing, looked at me and said: "Did you enjoy yourself last night? Did the staff sergeant behave himself?"

Without hesitation I answered: "He did nothing that I did not approve of, Sir. We had a lovely walk in the evening sun."

"Did you? I sent you both off an hour early at five o'clock and when I got back at ten the Bedford was still missing. What on earth did you do in all that time? The heathland starts just the other side of the railway crossing. You were there in ten minutes." He turned over sheet after sheet and went on with his signing without looking up. "It is none of my business. I'm just curious."

I had to think fast. "Well, Sir, you know we did not have coupons for a meal out. There is no privacy in the office, and the hours just fly when you enjoy each others` company, and before it was dark we played hide and seek."

He looked up abruptly and I thought his moustache ends were drooping more than usual. "Did you say 'hide and seek'?"

"I don't know what the Scots call it. You would know that, being a Scotsman, Sir." He looked very angry now, but he should have known that I was not trying to make fun of him. How should I know what words a Scotsman uses or what games he plays.

"They call it the bloody same, Miss Schiel, only adults don't play that game in Scoootland," he shouted. His fist came crushing down on his desk. His head went red. I had obviously said the wrong thing, but what should I have said. The 'tomato kiss with promise' was too private, the proposal – I could not have told him about that. I looked at him. He just sat there enjoying his superiority in our contest of wits. Finally I just straightened up, drew a deep breath and said with all the confidence I could muster:

"You are quite right, Sir, but I never had a conventional childhood and if that is so, the natural desires of a child may want to assert themselves in later life. I can't even remember having ever played that game as a child and there, in that open heathland, nature was so beautiful that I wanted to be a child again with no commitments. As a man with a wide range of experiences you would surely understand that people, wherever they come from, do stupid things at times because they are upset, happy or because no-one is looking. What did you want me to tell you? That the staff sergeant and I had planned to elope or that we had a flaming row? Nothing like that happened last night, unless it happened in your vivid imagination, if you will excuse my frankness, Sir."

There was a brief silence. He probably realised that at that time certain things in my life were private. Full stop. He slowly walked over to me. He put out his hand which I shook and he said: "I hope you and Ernest will be very happy. I really do." I could only muster: "Thank you, Sir." We were all smiles again. I had saved the situation and he had apologised for having lost his temper. The major never mentioned the incident to Ernest.

Now a married couple, we walked through the heathland arm in arm. There were still some war time souvenirs to be found if you looked hard enough, but the area had been pretty well cleaned up. We looked forward to returning to our new home in Omagh. The boat had left the lounge, the window was back in place and two second hand armchairs made it possible to sit by the fire. We were winning, as the saying goes and a couple of years later our son, Douglas, was born.

13.

We enjoyed our time in Omagh. I was still dressmaking when Douglas crawled about the floor, building ships with empty cotton reels. Another few years passed and I was asked to join the design staff of the local shirt factory. They were now producing men's beach-wear and pyjamas for the London market. I accepted the job for a short trial period but left soon afterwards. I could manage dressmaking with a baby and a seamstress, as long as I stayed at home. I could not go out to work.

A few years later Ernest was transferred back to England. He had to sort out some office mismanagement at the firm's Carlisle branch and would be extremely busy for a few months. It would be an important move for him and it was decided that I should take the boy to my parents for a while until things settled down again. It was a hectic time. I gave up all dressmaking and only finished what had been started. The house was emptied, the furniture put into storage awaiting shipment because from now on we would live in premises provided by the firm and have our expenses paid.

It all worked very well. Douglas and I moved to Germany for about two months and Ernest showed his potential in Carlisle by working very hard and for long hours which was only possible without any other commitments. We had been very reluctant to agree to that arrangement, to agree to such a long separation, but we felt it was the price we had to pay for not having been able to complete our education soon after we had left school. It was a red-letter-day when we were all united again, making a new home in Carlisle. We now lived in the centre of a big town. Ernest was still very busy, still working late and deep down I knew we were both longing to be back in Ireland.

When we were finally asked if we would like to move back to Ireland we both jumped for joy. Ernest started work in Castledawson and we moved into a firm's house beside the factory. The neighbours were very friendly. We could relax and enjoy the countryside, visit friends in Donegal and do little jobs about the house. A trip to Belfast was to be a special surprise for me. Ernest bought me a Bechstein piano which would be my pride and joy for as long as I lived in Ireland. I already had a piano in Wiltshire but sold it before we first moved to Ireland. It had served its purpose and was all we could afford at that time. Now I started playing again and really enjoying it. For once I was 'a lady of leisure', but not for long.

We had a new idea for a part-time job which was less exacting than the dressmaking. We bought old, dilapidated caravans, gave them a new look and refurbished them. Ernest was just the right man to check the chassis and braking system. It was not hard to hold and use a paintbrush, to develop a flare for interior design and perhaps recover soft furnishings. With those jobs attended to, the transformation was complete. The price tag changed dramatically, we could take a well deserved rest and somewhere in the corner of the factory yard stood a 'new' caravan for sale. As time progressed we managed to purchase and complete a caravan in such a way that we also let it at Portrush in July and August before we offered it for sale. It was the best idea we had had for a long time. All my black market skills were reborn for I was the one who had to get rid of the article in the end and I enjoyed it. Later, when we owned a plot of land at the outskirts of Castledawson, we had two or three caravans of later designs and stored them there until that sideline also came to an end.

14.

I t would appear that I was barred from entering East Germany, but I managed to secure a visa from the Polish authorities for a visit to Treptow, now Trzebiatow and now in Poland. I will have to get used to calling the town by its Polish name, the town I called snob's island when I went to school there. The obvious access would have been via East Germany, but I had to think of other ways of entering the country. I flew to Denmark and boarded a Polish ship to Swinoujscie (Swinemünde).

The Polish sailors would remember the exact date. One of their nationals had slipped off the ship during the voyage. I had watched him clamber along the port side with a sheer drop into the sea. His intention was probably to surprise a girlfriend behind one of the port holes. There was hardly a hand-hold and only a precarious foot-hold. He slipped and fell into the sea, about twenty metres below him. As it turned out, he could hardly swim more than two or three strokes. I could not speak Polish, but I screamed and pointed into the sea to alert other passengers and then watched a most efficient rescue operation at sea. The co-ordination between the captain on board and the first officer in the life boat was perfect and so was the after-care of the casualty. No life was lost and every passenger there must have wondered how an adult could have been so careless. When I last saw him his face still had the green colour of the sea. The problem had been the condition of the sea. It was rough. The captain could see the casualty from his bridge. The life boat crew could not. They had to wait for instructions from the bridge. The captain, on the other hand, had to avoid drifting away from the scene for fear of losing sight of the casualty altogether. Every now and then I heard the engines cut in briefly while the ship edged towards the life boat, and every now and then I had a glimpse of the man thrashing about in the foaming water. They had everything under perfect control and I had never witnessed such a spectacular operation. Thank goodness it had happened in daylight.

All the landing facilities worked smoothly when we disembarked in the morning and a line of taxi drivers hoped for business. I was impressed by the general efficiency and had also a foretaste of the Polish economy. Before I left home I had learned that Polish money was worth very little and that I would be well advised to take West German marks and coffee. I had been a hardened black-marketeer at one time and needed no picture painted of the Polish economy.

I hailed the first driver and asked the price of a run to Trzebiatow and back, a distance of over a hundred miles. I used sign language and the name of the town. To my surprise he spoke some English. The option of staying for a few days had occurred to me but was soon rejected, because I was a total stranger without any knowledge of the language. He told me, it was not the first time he had taken a passenger to Trzebiatow and back. The charge would be five pounds sterling and one pound of coffee. I felt I just had to increase that amount somewhat and gave him what spare cash I had in my purse.

The roads seemed well maintained with sporadic traffic of Soviet military vehicles and every five or ten minutes an old Polish car or van. The driver was quite chatty in a friendly way and I was staggered at the level of poverty which existed in Poland. Treptow had been a town of some 10,000 inhabitants. He said that there were now about 5,000 Poles living in Trzebiatow.

On arrival there I invited the driver to the best lunch he could find. He was a thin man in his middle forties and looked as though he could do with a square meal. He parked at the only restaurant in the town and ordered the most expensive meal, a small burger on a piece of dry bread for the equivalent of a few pence. He relished it but could not manage a second helping. For a special treat he drove me the few miles to Deep at the Baltic Sea where we as pupils had battled with the currents in a school rowing boat. Finally I asked him if I could have a couple of hours on my own, before we would have to leave Trzebiatow for the evening boat to Denmark. He agreed immediately and for a while we went our separate ways.

My first call had to be 'our' house; at least it would by now have belonged to my sister and to me. War damage could be seen but only in the outside plaster. The three flats were occupied and I boldly ventured into the garden at the back. At first I noticed that the three outside toilets were still in use. So no Polish council had finished laying sewerage pipes, probably because there were none to be bought.

I then approached the garden gate and revelled at the sight of prime vegetables and fruit in season growing in this fertile soil. For a keen gardener like myself, it was a joy to behold, but after living on a four- acre site in Ireland, I thought this little Polish garden was minute. It might have measured a quarter of an acre or even less. During the war it had meant survival for our family, not only with its fruit and vegetables for our consumption but also with its produce for bartering. It was our little gold mine.

Behind my back a window on the first floor of the house had opened and a woman's voice called in German, "I no sell, only if coffee". Black market jargon had survived and involuntarily I had to laugh. "I no want, I no coffee, I look," I called back. My coffee was in the car and, in any case, I had already promised to give it to the taxi driver. She and I knew now where we stood and an arm-waving gesture told me to clear off. I was trespassing, I know, and I could not explain because I could not speak Polish. Eventually I was compensated by the German government for the loss of my share in the house, now in Poland. It came to £ 100 and was the down-payment for our first privately owned property in Castledawson. I would not have squandered a penny of it.

On the way back to the town centre I passed a kiosk beside the road. It was the town's clothes shop; at least I saw no other. Inside stood a large table heaped with ladies' and gents' garments. A patient queue fingered and filed past it. If a customer found what he or she wanted, payments were made outside the entrance. There the proprietor sat on a chair in the sunshine. No-one would have dreamt of stealing anything. No-one was different, richer or poorer than anyone else. The people had been refugees from the South of Poland. They were ordered by the Soviet Union to leave their country, a strip of land henceforth to be part of Russia. I saw no signs of snobbery or subservience in the town, which had given me so much grief when I lived there and I wished them well. I would never have wanted to live in that town again anyway. In normal times my sister and I would have sold the property, now it was the price we paid for a lost war.

The shops in the centre of the town were mostly empty, at least the shelves were. The supermarket had a row of tins of beetroot and a few buckets and bowls for sale, but when I gesticulated that I was looking for something to eat, the assistant pointed to Friday on the calendar. I took that to mean that food was expected to arrive on Friday.

My old grammar school had another level of classrooms added and was now an elementary school. There was no time to go inside the school but, who knows, I thought I might be back one day.

The last call before joining my taxi driver was to a block of flats where we had always waited for the maths teacher on a winter's Saturday night. He had regularly taken us out for a session on 'the sky at night' and his lessons were always most enjoyable. Some people can command the attention of a crowd and some cannot. He could. I now found the flats all occupied, in total disrepair and all private entrance doors were closed with a piece of string round a nail. I left quickly. Maybe there was time to catch a glimpse of the river, that river we had enjoyed in the school's rowing boats. I stood there in a state of disbelief. Gone were the boats' house, the varnished 'fours' and, of course, the caretaker. Slime covered the banks. A narrow, half over-grown, polluted stream moved sluggishly towards the Baltic. The place stank or did I only imagine that? I hurried towards the market square. It had all been too much for me. I tried to focus on the town hall. There had to be a red car, a driver waiting for me. The Poles were so honest. He would not leave me in this dump. My over-night bag was in the car too. I had wanted to show trust. I briefly sat down on a low wall beside the school and then I saw the car. There was no hurry. I had plenty of time. When I got to the car I smiled at the driver: "Did you have a little rest after all your driving?" He nodded and said: "We must go now, in case we have a puncture on the way."

All went well until we were nearly at the docks. Then the car gave up. My driver hailed another taxi. I said I would walk because I had no more ready cash or goods. I protested in a mixture of French and English. "Please, drop me here." The two drivers took no notice of me. My bag was transferred and I was bundled into another taxi for the last few hundred yards. "I have nothing to give you. What I have I would need for my fare to Germany!" I shouted. He stopped at the boarding office and turned to face me. "I don't want anything. Have a good trip and remember us in your prayers." I put my arms round him, a complete stranger, and said, "I will". Everything went so quickly then until I was on board. I flopped down in the first arm chair I came to and prayed, "Dear God, can I go anywhere without crying my heart out? Please help the Poles to have an honourable place in Europe where they can get the things which we take for granted. Amen." Presently I got up and went on deck, mentally digesting what I had seen and heard that day. The German province of Pommern had gone. In time the houses would decay, the language had already disappeared. Outside the harbour the Soviet war ships were at anchor. What were they doing here, anyway? The Polish navy should have been there instead and then I remembered. Europe was not completely at peace yet, not as long as the Polish Solidarity movement gathered momentum and annoyed its big neighbour.

15.

It was on this boat trip to Poland, particularly on the return journey, that I gazed across the Baltic Sea and dozens of memories of my mother flooded back into my mind. She was the only one of us alive who had suffered lasting psychological damage in the immediate post-war period.

True, we had lost all our possessions and had to start all over again, but outwardly we were alive and well. We never talked about the war years if we could help it, never mentioned Trautchen's name. We might have lingered by her picture on the wall, but that was all. We were simply afraid that my mother would burst into tears unable to stop crying. Her experiences had left her morose at best and ready to cry out loud, quite uncontrollably, at worst. The reason was not so much the loss of her daughter. It was what I called the after-effects of Trautchen's death. She permanently blamed herself for having gambled with the lives of her three daughters, for each one of us could have died because of her decision to leave the peaceful British zone of occupation in Lüneburg for Berlin's last stand in the war. As it was, she only lost my little sister, but that was enough to break her heart irretrievably. She had faithfully promised me to wait in Lüneburg for my return from a nursing course. Being a refugee, the relatives had to take her in, but whatever happened there she broke her promise. What followed in Berlin was a succession of predictable calamities which she was unable to control. All was peaceful when she arrived in the city. Everyone was just waiting for the earth to erupt under the Soviet bombardment and when it did she could no longer cope. Whether anyone had told her that she had killed her child, I do not know. They may have done, although I prefer to think that she went through spells of insanity.

Ernest and I happened to be in Brighton when she was taken into hospital in Heidelberg. She had not been well lately and I contacted my father from Brighton who told me the bad news. She had cancer in its last stages and no more than a few weeks to live. We altered our plans immediately. Ernest travelled home towing a caravan which we had just bought and I booked my passage to Germany at Dover.

When I arrived in hospital the doctor confirmed the bad news. I told my father that, if he wanted to, he could take a well deserved rest now. I was there and would visit my mother daily. Maybe he would like to visit Eka who had just given birth to her first son in another hospital in the same town. Or maybe he would like to make his visits shorter with me there, he had the choice. Except for short meal breaks I stayed with my mother all day every day and towards the end I spent two nights with her as well. During the last night I slipped into bed with her and cradled her in my arms. She was so grateful, and I knew what she was thinking. *If only she could have done as much for Trautchen,* but she was prevented from doing so, for Trautchen lay in an isolation ward. She could not even see her mother. Even the nurses were reluctant to enter the child's room and when they did it was only very briefly. I have always been very close to my mother and I told her so again before she finally closed her eyes and drifted into another world. I said a short prayer, kissed her good-bye, got up and rang for the nurse. I was so pleased that I could share the last precious moments with her and that I could take over from Eka and my father when they needed my help most. Finally I crept into a corner of the hospital to let the tears flow freely.

16.

The Berlin Wall was still standing, maintained and fortified as if to last for ever and West Berlin remained just a very small island surrounded by East Germany. I mention that because this fact became a yardstick by which we measured event, time and place if we could not remember the date. At that time Ernest and I enjoyed a holiday with my parents in Schleswig Holstein, in the north of Germany. The start of this account dates back to the end of the war when my mother was still well and had learned from the Red Cross that her brother Fredrick had returned from Russia. He was in Germany again after years of captivity in Siberia as prisoner of war. We had brought our car over to help look for the missing relative and finally help unite the siblings. The trouble was, at that time he had no fixed address. His story, when we finally located him, is far more moving than anything I have ever written or experienced, but he was only interested in sharing it with his family. It is for that reason that I have altered names and places, although I personally like to be reminded of the misery and suffering which can befall families when war rages through their country. I have heard of worse cases, but not of more unusual ones.

Uncle Fredrick had once escaped from the salt mines in Siberia only to be denounced and recaptured at the German border. He was sent back to Siberia and worked there until he was no longer fit to work. He was then discharged and handed documents to give him free passage to the West German border where he arrived some months later. The rags he stood up in were his only possessions. He was pushed from one refugee camp to another until the Red Cross secured a one-bedroom flat for him and a carer who called at regular intervals. She was a German refugee from the new Polish territory and he married her after a while.

Over a period of years she restored his health and strength and they were very happy.

When we arrived on the scene there was great jubilation. We helped him get established in his new home by buying, amongst other things, a second-hand double bed and mattress and he was so grateful at the prospects of sleeping in a bed, not having had that pleasure for over ten years. We felt totally embarrassed. Ernest grew extremely fond of him and everyone was delighted when Fredrick and his wife eventually moved to the Heidelberg area where my parents lived. From now on we met the whole family every time we went to Germany. Fredrick often talked about his son, Robert, and he read the Red Cross newsletter religiously in the hope of finding his son alive, the son he had to leave at boarding school when he received his call-up papers at the beginning of the war.

We now know that towards the end of the war the headmaster of the boarding school had simply opened the door and told the children to walk home, westwards. The Soviet army would be on their heels shortly. The kids would be overrun, but there would be nothing he, the headmaster, could do to change the situation. Each child was given a bag of food and the headmaster's good wishes. Robert was not quite twelve at the time. He assumed rightly that his father would be a prisoner of war. So he set off to find his mother in Berlin. His parents were divorced. A 200-mile journey on foot brought him to Berlin and he did find his mother, but whether her partner made Robert's life a misery or no-one had time for him, I do not know. Robert was a very sensitive boy. He simply picked up a small blanket and some provisions and he set off into the extensive woods north of Berlin.

At that time those woods were bursting with Soviet encampments, right round the city. The soldiers were all waiting for the bombardment to start and for the order to storm into the city with fixed bayonets. For Robert life was not worth living any more. He reached the woods and sat down beside one of the Soviet tents, ate his sandwiches and drank his lemonade. He was tired, lay down and pulled the blanket over him. He had crept there unnoticed by the soldiers whose field glasses were only focussed on the city in the distance. When Robert woke up the soldiers had gathered round him and some stranger offered him a bowl of soup. There were smiles all round and lots of jolly sounding words which Robert did not understand, but he made up his mind to stay. In my experience Soviet soldiers were always kind to children.

I cannot remember how long he lived in those woods, but I do remember looking him up in a town not far from where I was nursing. He must have been about fourteen years old at that time. I had spotted his name in a Red Cross index of refugees from the East. He was cleaning windows at the time, was thin and shy and frightened to be seen talking to me. I confronted his foster-mother and wanted to know why Robert had to work without being fed. He had a ration card the same as anyone else and why did the boy have so many bruises. I was clearly upset. I even discussed Robert's dilemma with the matron in the hospital and we both tried to invent some kind of job for him at the hospital, unpaid, of course, because of his age. At least he would be fed and maybe find a paid job later. At this time he could hardly read or write. When I called at the Red Cross with those proposals in mind I was accompanied by a representative of the charity to the house where Robert lived. By then the boy had absconded and his foster-mother was taken into custody for neglecting the child. There was no trace of him.

Years later Ernest and I met him in Fredrick`s home. The father had found his son and also gained a grandson. Like Robert, his wife had drifted through life. She had lost her parents and, as far as I knew, had not been to any school. She could not cope with a baby and one day she was gone. No-one in our family has seen her again. A solution had to be found to the problems of that family. Robert secured an unskilled job in a factory and Fredrick and his wife brought up the baby, their grandson. Some time after that they all moved to the north of Germany and we somehow lost contact. It was around 1980 that I was sent their address and made plans to visit them.

Fredrick and his wife were in their late seventies now and they went to so much trouble to welcome me that I could not keep the tears back. He had waited all day at the window to catch the first glimpse of me. She had spent all day preparing meals and getting my bed ready. I can but say it was a super holiday. After dinner I had to see all the photographs of Robert and the baby, then the baby as a teenager and finally at his graduation ceremony in the university.

I was turning over pages in their photograph album when the door bell rang. Fredrick's wife opened the door and in stormed a handsome, tall young man in frayed jeans, a broken shoe lace in his hand. He hugged his grandmother: "Oma, have you got another shoe lace for me?" With that he gave her a gym shoe and half a shoe lace. Oma would know what to do with the shoe and with the tear-away she had brought up since he was a baby. Then he hugged his grandfather and finally he faced me. We quickly sized each other up and within seconds were also in each other's arms. We spent a lovely evening together. He told me all about his wife and two small children at present in their caravan at the Baltic Sea, but he had to come and meet me. It struck me that he was extremely happy every time he visited his grandparents. There was also a loving contact with his father. I asked him still in German whether he enjoyed his work and he explained to me in perfect English what his duties were as the youngest member in an international firm of prominent lawyers. I have wonderful memories of that day.

When Ernest and I called at Fredrick`s home a year or two later he had passed away and the young people were abroad. We had just lived that little bit too far apart to come more often. A few months later a neighbour informed us that Fredrick`s wife, Norma, had also died.

In retrospect, Robert and his wife were the losers. They could not adjust to Germany`s relative affluence in those days, to a society of hard working men and women who could read and write and who would throw things away because they were outdated. He refused to live near his son because he did not want to be a burden on the family. Thinking back, Robert was my only playmate during our holidays in Treptow when he and Uncle Fredrick visited us. Admittedly he was younger than I, but he was always game to try something new and he was daring as long as I was there as well to catch him before he fell, or pull him to safety before he drowned. I do not have his address. He had long since given up writing or receiving mail. I simply lost contact − sadly. Robert had become an outsider, a recluse, another kind of war victim and, I suppose the same had applied to his wife. I do not know where they had met. It would not surprise me if it was in some woodland, begging for food in nearby villages, or even stealing at times. Robert will probably also have passed away by now. It had hardly been a life worth living and yet he passed on such precious genes to his son.

17.

During the winter I still visited my father every year. He came to us in the summer and we now spent more time in Donegal boating. We had also started building a bungalow on our four-acre plot of woodland in Castledawson. There had been a dwelling on the site, but we gradually demolished it to make room for the bungalow, garage and a large shed. It housed Ernest's workshop, a small office and whatever boat we had at the time. We could also wheel the boat out and push in a caravan if it required outside work on a rainy day. Living in the firm's house, there was no pressure put on us to complete the bungalow in record time. For the first few stages we had employed a bricklayer at weekends or evenings and Ernest worked alongside him. We all gave a hand at times especially Douglas. I suppose we had in mind to make a home for our retirement or, in case the firm wanted us to move to another town or country, to have the option of staying in Castledawson. We were now no longer willing to leave Ireland.

Trying to manage a four-acre site with a large garden and large bungalow with generous amenities, which we never had time to use, was probably the worst mistake we had made in our lives. We should have sold all but half an acre. That would have been enough for all our needs, but we were both to blame for the shortcomings in our planning. At the time, extensive grounds were most desirable and we had always loved wide open spaces. To own them was an extra bonus, but at the same time a bottomless pit we had dug for ourselves.

I was looking now for a sideline of a different kind to occupy me in the daytime, for we only went evenings to the 'estate' or the *joint,* as we called it. This sideline, which I am now referring to, should have occurred to me years ago. In a neighbouring village a

Belgian lady had found a job giving French conversation lessons at the nearby grammar school and I envied her. I would have loved to give lessons in German conversation. That must have been passed on to the headmaster who subsequently contacted me with that offer in mind.

I knew that the pay would be poor because I was not qualified. Nevertheless, I became a teacher. Sitting on one of their desks, I just merged with a group of my A-level students and picked a subject like barber, dentist or a shopping expedition and we turned the situation into a little play. I had written some of the relative words on the blackboard and now there was no more English spoken. The boys and girls had to confront whom they had 'come to see' in German. Cries like "I don`t know how to say that in German" soon echoed round the room. To which I simply replied: "*Ich verstehe nur deutsch*" (I only understand German), or "*dann frage mich auf deutsch*" (then ask me in German). Quite hilarious situations developed because the students were too reluctant to attempt a conversation although they were very good in German generally. I had to recall some of Miss Understood's methods and eventually we all enjoyed the lessons as the students became less inhibited. In time we discussed a German poem or German prose for which they had prepared at home. At the end of the lesson there was always a snap question like: "What do you say if a policeman accuses you of shop lifting?" or "What do you do if you have lost your passport in Germany?"

After a couple of months the headmaster wanted to see me again. "Have you thought of qualifying as a teacher?" he asked. I had done so many times, of course, but with a small child at home I could not enter a three year course at university. With Douglas at school now it was a different matter, but I would still have to prepare and sit for an English language examination. I had only studied English as a foreign language.

At home I told Ernest about my interview. "Why not teach music instead of German?" he asked. "You could prepare for your diploma at home and once you had that, you told me the other day, you would only need one year at a teacher training college." So that is what I did. It was inevitable that my piano playing had got rusty and it was a nuisance that some of the notes had different names in English, but I could overcome that. Fis, B und H now had to be translated into F sharp, B flat and B respectively. I found a wonderful piano teacher in Belfast and when he wanted me to make a correction and play E flat, I reeled off the English names of the notes in my mind before I could play it. He soon gave up that game and simply pointed to the key on the piano giving me time to adjust mentally. Gradually I learned the notes like a small child does and never thought of mentioning the German names again. It was too confusing. I drove to Belfast for lessons once a fortnight, became a Licentiate of Trinity College London and after attending a training college for a year I applied for my first qualified teaching post. It could be done, but I was sorely missed by the family, although I always came home at weekends. I could have done all that in Germany after I had left school, but I was not granted that opportunity.

It was not surprising that I could not find employment nearer home, but it was important that I did not waste too much time looking for a job. I had to start somewhere and hoped gradually to make my way towards the desired position in the desired location. I accepted a position in a special school in Whiteabbey as music and form-teacher of the most senior class and loved it. I taught a multitude of subjects, certainly all the required subjects, but I placed the greatest emphasis on whether the children enjoyed the lessons. The boring parts were kept short and sweet and what they really enjoyed had to involve learning of a different kind. They became much less inhibited by learning as they played. The classroom had an open annex with shelves which I curtained off in such a way as would leave room for a puppet theatre. I procured a selection of puppets which you operated by slipping a hand into them and moving them as you acted their part. Suffice to say, I wrote the first plays, the children gradually took over from me. They readily performed for staff and pupils to screams of laughter or genuine tears. I even had the idea of having some of their plays published. I often wondered what had made those shows so successful and I think it was because the children were not seen during the performance. They were not judged, not criticised as they acted. They were just themselves and they let go. That alone would not have justified those activities, but it also gave them the confidence to do much better in English and general knowledge. They no longer crept into a corner or hid behind the girl in front. They met strangers on equal terms and that was important in their last year at school.

After a year at Whiteabbey and tiresome bus journeys I was offered a job as music teacher of a secondary school in Belfast. It still meant a long journey from Castledawson and back every day, but that post would one day give me a better chance to secure a similar one nearer home. It did so after another year in Belfast. For me, the highlight of that year was the performance of Schubert's German Mass in a Belfast church by my choir. I had translated the work into English and the children did really well. That year also came to an end and I started work at a school in Magherafelt, four miles from home.

Belfast, which I had grown to like, left a sad mark on me. I taught there during the troubles without really understanding all the reasons for and the historic background to the unrests. I had the music room window smashed, bricks with abusive messages thrown at an expensive piano. I had my way to school barred by some ruffians questioning my right to use the pavement. There seemed to be no rule of law and when law breaks down you finish up with Hitler's kind of patriotism. I was promised that no harm would come to me, but who could promise such protection?

I tried to compare the problems here with my experiences in main land Europe. The Poles were now resettled in what was my country. They had moved into my house because we had lost the war. To confuse matters further, the Poles had themselves been expelled from their country by the Russians and clearing out former citizens, before moving in, seemed to be the done thing. That would at least ensure that future generations would always win at the ballot box. Patriotism can achieve wonderful results in sport and music, industry and education, but Hitler's patriotism tolerated no compromise and that was Germany's downfall. I feared that Ireland might go the same way, if the Irish could not settle their differences. Perpetuating hatred gets you nowhere not in Poland nor in Ireland and one does not have to give up patriotism to live peacefully, one only needs to discard the wrong patriotism and sometimes see the other person's point of view. I have seen many signs of that happening then and now and I congratulate those people who have taken up the challenge and who held out the hand of friendship. It is not painful. I have tried it in Poland. It is very rewarding.

18.

Eventually the Berlin Wall came down. The Soviet regime collapsed and if you wanted to, and had the money, you could go anywhere in Europe. When I listened to news broadcasts I could not believe them, not then, not the day after. There had to be a hitch. The news was so earth-shattering that it took time to sink in.

On one of my visits to my father I diverted to Berlin. Without hindrance I could now cross into East Berlin. Ella, my old piano teacher would be dead by now. I crossed nevertheless because I had spent the formative years of my life in East Berlin.

My sister, Eka, was at my side and we relived the past together. I climbed the stairs of the familiar block of flats and knocked on the door of my erstwhile home. She decided to wait outside. When was I last standing here? It was after my long walk to and through Berlin. The city looked different now. It had risen from the dead. Hollow footsteps approached the door. A painter and decorator opened it. There was a strong smell of paint.

"Who are you?" he addressed me. "The place is not supposed to be ready until next week."

"A spirit of the past, that's me." I shook his hand. "I used to live here."

"Pleased to meet you. The last lot only stayed for two years."

"I'm talking about 50 years ago," I corrected him.

He scratched his head and said no more, but he let me roam through the empty rooms. From the living room window I had a view of the cemetery where Trautchen was buried. I turned my head to the left and murmured: "And here stood my piano."

My thoughts drifted back to my piano teacher, Ella. I knew so little about her. She was a slight, elderly, elegant lady who could have been anything between forty and sixty years old when I regularly went to her for lessons. She was revered in the community and could play the piano like no-one else. People used to stand on the pavement underneath the music room window, just listening. Any informer could and probably did pass her bungalow to check whether she was at home or away. More often than not she would play when she had finished giving lessons, but it would appear she was always one step ahead of her informer.

She knew that I had lost my two Jewish friends because I had finally come to her for clarification of their disappearance. As far as I can recall, at that time she could not help me either, or was it she would not, to protect me and her. I was very young and had only recently started going to grammar school. I would not have understood what an informer was and what the consequences of his or her work were likely to be. Then, after her boating accident, she came to me with her problem. By that time I was much older. Our relationship had deepened and she probably felt she could trust me, but Ella only asked if my parents would let me go to a Jewish teacher for lessons. She stressed that it would be important occasionally to fake her presence in the house and then she paused to gauge my reaction to her request. I did not have to ask my parents and agreed there and then.

Standing now within the walls of my former home, I suddenly realised that my new teacher had been at least as brilliant a piano player as Ella was. What did that mean? It meant that any informer listening outside to the music coming from the inside must have thought that Ella was at home when she was not. With hindsight she had found a unique alibi for her dubious activities. That, coupled with generous donations to the party had kept her and her charges safe. Who, I had asked myself, were these charges? I can only surmise that one of them was a concert pianist, my new piano teacher after Ella's boating accident – perhaps a friend of Ella's during her student days? How many friends did Ella protect? I know no answer to that question either, there were no eyewitnesses, only hearsay and her guarded remarks to me. Her friends would have left as soon as it was safe, maybe even under military escort. Who, in the last days of the war and first days of peace, would have taken notice of some huddled figures slipping away in some Soviet car or even on foot? The streets would have been empty. All citizens stayed down below in cellars, all except Ella – perhaps.

Ella would readily have told me all the answers, if I had asked her on my last visit to Berlin, if I had taken the trouble to walk from where I stood now to Ella's house, but when I was here, in this very room, I had come to rescue my mother and Eka. I was afraid to risk the few extra steps and call on Ella for all our sakes. "Shame on me," I cried, put my hands in front of my face and slid down the corner of the wall. I curled up in a heap on the floor – in tears. I felt so ashamed of myself, not having called on Ella. I was not aware of the present time, only the circumstances 50 years ago. Of course, the thought had occurred to me to visit Ella, but I had the responsibility of two charges then, I kept repeating. Any deviation from my plan, any walk through empty streets with just a military presence, was not safe. I tried to justify my cowardice. "That's why I had crept through the cemetery to come here," I was sobbing. "Mother, anyone getting caught or failing to report for work... you know yourself, you absconded... would have been deported. What should I have done?" I thought I felt my mother's hand stroking my head, as though she was saying: "You did just right."

My mother had died a long time ago. I closed my eyes, at first never noticing the devil looking round the corner. He had a smirk on his distorted face. "You would find a lot of excuses. I didn't expect anything else. You could have done more, but you didn't want to. You were scared. End of story."

"Leave me alone," I screamed and shook my head from side to side- - - -. Presently I opened my eyes and looked at my watch. "Oh Lord," I whispered and stood up. My clothes were filthy.

The voice of the painter called out, "Are you all right?" "Coming", I answered in a similar tone of voice. After a quick 'brush-up' I dried my face, emerged from my hide-out and thanked the painter. I also left a box of chocolates which was intended for the tenant, but it did not matter now.

"You look kind of dishevelled," my sister greeted me outside. "Is everything all right?"

"Yes, of course, there is some painting and decorating going on upstairs," I remarked casually. "Sorry I was so long."

We walked in silence for a while and briefly sat on one of the seats in the courtyard. Eka read a book and I just dozed. One other occasion came to mind when Ella gave a coffee party in her music room – standing room only. Invited were teaching staff (not Miss Understood) of the two local grammar schools, a few senior piano pupils and parents and representatives of Nazi top brass. Among the teaching staff were definitely some members of dubious political views but as yet only under observation. Suddenly Ella's high-pitched voice rang out: "Frau Schiel, it is too early to go home. We are all Nazis having a wonderful time." Right enough, the gentleman in SS uniform, glancing in Ella's direction, looked extremely happy. He had provided the coffee, since no-one else could buy any. He also remembered, no doubt, Ella's immediate agreement to stop playing and teaching all Mahler's and Mendelssohn's music, since those two gentlemen were of Jewish origin. Ella confided in me a different version of events when she showed me a poster explaining the new law. She was furious, but she was a strong woman and she knew how to get her priorities right. Her dark eyes sparkled when she faced me: "Make no mistake, a temporary shut-down, one day we'll open up all the stops again WITH Mendelssohn and Mahler."

It was time I stopped day-dreaming and left the courtyard. I walked to the cemetery with Eka. She was eleven years old when she had attended the funeral of Trautchen. Maybe she could not remember where the grave was, maybe it had been re-excavated to accommodate the body of someone else. We could not find it but said our prayers all the same, addressing some cross with another name of a war- time child.

"I would like to have one last look at the spot where Ella's bungalow had once stood," I said quietly. "It's on the way to our B&B place." So we left that part of our past for good —I thought, but as things turned out I walked down a very similar memory lane a few years later with my son.

I seemed to remember that there were two or three bungalows of exactly the same design in Parkstraße, but only as seen from the front. I never saw the rear view of any of them. They stood close together with, I think, a narrow passage between them. They all had a small cellar window at the front, level with the pavement and a large room and hall with the front door above it. In Ella`s case it was a large music room and a small milk and cheese shop, the latter approachable by a flight of concrete steps and at the back leading to a dark corridor and a door to the music room. We always approached the music room via the shop and as we did so we, as small children, had to curtsy to whoever was serving there and utter a happy sounding "Good day". Such were Ella's instructions until we were old enough to be addressed by the unfamiliar form of *Sie* instead of *Du*.

I do not think anyone knew what was at the back of the building except Ella. Her mother might have known, but she had long since died. It had always been a high-walled, small property with a lot of privacy and was accepted as such. On rare occasions she talked about an outhouse where she stored obsolete furniture. I suspect that there was a connection between the cellar and the outhouse, a passage under one of the bedrooms at cellar level. All windows had at all times heavy net curtains drawn including the cellar window at the front. As a small child I remember having tried to peep in there. I also remember that at one time a burglar had removed the iron bars from the front cellar window to get access to the inside of the bungalow. He was apparently apprehended by Ella. There was such a fuss created until the council gave her permission to have the cellar window at the front bricked up. She would not have needed permission to have that work done, but she wanted everyone to know that it was done officially for her own safety and that of her pupils.

Now, I am of the opinion that the whole incident of the break-in was rigged up by Ella to create a legitimate reason for the alteration to her bungalow, certainly not for a safer environment to suit some Jewish friends. No-one would have suspected such incredible behaviour, because had that been vaguely rumoured, she and her friends would have been arrested within minutes. As it was, the alteration made life easier for the people living in the bungalow. Ella had two personalities and played whatever part was required to perfection. Deep down she was convinced that Hitler would not survive for long and that gave her the strength to play her double-part for so long.

Having walked past the newly built flats now occupying the site of Ella's bungalow, I wondered why the other two owners had kept their bungalows. I suppose Ella could no longer maintain her property and she had no heir. Some estate agent must have solved the problem to his advantage. I called on the lady living at number 12. Did she know any more about the bungalow or owner of No.11? She told me that the building was demolished when a row of four-storey apartments was built. "As you see, the last house of the row sits in my back yard," the owner of No.

12 complained. She paused for a minute and then went on: "I understand they gave the piano player a flat, but that is fifteen or twenty years in the past, and we only moved here two years ago."

It was probably as far as I could get with my enquiries and we headed for our lodgings. Of course Eka knew Ella as well. At some stage she was her pupil too, but when I started giving lessons, she was transferred to me – a cheaper option.

"How did Ella react when we moved from Berlin to Treptow?" asked Eka.

"She was devastated and hugged me as though I was her own child. She took the gold watch off her wrist and put it on mine. We just sat there crying."

"What happened to the watch?" Eka wanted to know.

"I wore it every day. During my time in the *Arbeitsdienst* I took it to Schlawe for repair and never had a chance to collect it. It was ready long before we fled to the West." After my refusal to become a leader within the *Arbeitsdienst* set-up I was only allowed to go to work and not into nearby towns. The farmer had been informed to that effect. He had to report me if I left the farm, and if he wanted to go on getting free labour, he knew he had to do as he was told. At that time I had reached an all-time low: My own people were treating me like dirt and the Russian guns were blasting their shells towards us. I felt my life was not worth much in those days. My eyes had misted over. I reached for my handkerchief, and the rest of the way we walked in silence.

The owner of our B&B must have thought we had got lost when we apologised for having missed our afternoon coffee. She seemed to be used to her guests arriving or leaving late and I was pleased to have a chance to talk to her briefly because she was often hard to find.

"I understand, you once had a famous piano teacher living in this street," I began my probing again. She laughed. "When we moved here from Leipzig I was looking for a teacher. My daughter wanted to learn to play the piano. I found the right person practically on the doorstep. Well, almost the right teacher. She was old and peculiar and could frighten anybody. Hanna packed it up after a while."

That evening I learnt all there was to know about Ella. Towards the end she did not have many mature pupils, rather a large group of Russian and German smaller children. She must have been in her nineties when she finally gave up teaching and was indeed allocated a flat not far from her bungalow which was then pulled down. She lived in her one room and bathroom for a short while, having gone completely mad, and then died without a friend or carer having been near her.

"Did you know about some Jewish friends Ella had?" I asked another guest. "I heard something like that. It was immediately after the war, long before we arrived here. I heard that they went to a collection centre and left the country. Those poor souls had a habit of being invisible." Another story was that Ella played the piano when the Russians stormed into East Berlin. She had so often told me that in the end she would survive by playing the piano. I believe she told no-one about her Jewish friends because she felt, what other people did not know could not harm them, but in her regimented mind there had to be an escape valve. She needed an outsider she could trust and I, a sixteen-year-old girl, was that person she sometimes tried to confide in.

Eka and I went up to our rooms. That day we had really achieved very little, or had we? Once inside the room, I lowered my head and stared at the floor. "Good-bye, Ella, so sorry I was stupid enough to leave your watch out of sight. I should have known better." The subject which had haunted me for the best part of my life was now closed. I could do nothing to change any part of it. She was a credit to the nation. May she rest in peace.

19.

Our family was the most precious thing in our lives: just one son, Douglas, our daughter-in-law, Ann, and three grandchildren, Mair, Simon and Amy. Yes, we seemed to get ourselves into situations where we had taken on too much and could not finish and maintain what we had started. "We'll manage," was the war cry, but we did not seem to manage without help. That was where the family stepped in – when and where we needed them. I would like to think that, in time, we had learnt from our mistakes and managed our affairs a bit better. We were always busy, sometimes too busy, and sometimes we had got it wrong and regretted the tasks which we had loaded onto ourselves and at times onto the family. There was never any damage done, just precious time wasted.

Douglas was a social worker in Northern Ireland. Shortly after the Berlin Wall had fallen the conditions of the children in homes and on the streets of Romania were at length publicised and Douglas took leave from his work in Northern Ireland to go with his family for a year to Bucharest.

Ernest and I had now retired and were living near Carrick-on-Shannon, in the Republic of Ireland. Mail and phone calls were erratic – delayed and interrupted. In the end Ernest had the idea of visiting the family with a load of medical supplies, food and clothing for the street children. At first we could not pick and choose the gifts and said that we would accept items new or second hand for the age of four or five and older. We decided to drive there and I could hardly wait, but first there was much work to be done to organize such a journey.

I was asked what our true motives were to embark on such a venture. Was it a spirit of adventure, seeing the family again, a feeling of doing our bit to help, testing our response to a challenge or did we perhaps have a religious motive? To that I can honestly say that we wanted to see the family again. That was number one priority, but it seemed a good idea to make it a worthwhile trip in other respects. In time we became obsessed with the project, a tendency not altogether new in our lives. At no time did we begrudge the cost to ourselves.

The response of the public who heard about our plans was unbelievable. Everything was in short supply in Romania, so we had to be selective. It was more important for a child to have an operation than to receive a teddy bear to play with. At the time we owned a Volkswagen Passat Estate and a strong fire service trailer to which Ernest fitted a lockable lid. We completely gutted the rear of the car and fitted a net from behind our front seats to the ceiling, so that the cargo could not smother us in the front seats, when the brakes were put on. A new set of tyres was fitted all round, a special heavy duty type on the trailer. The documentation required was extremely detailed and we knew well which items were illegal and should not have been included in our load.

The involvement of the public started when I went into a shop and bought a large supply of underwear. Naturally, I had to reveal the reason for such a purchase. The lady who owned the shop became my most efficient helper. A big sign went up in her shop window and whoever made a purchase would also buy something for the Romanian box.

After a couple of weeks we had also collected 70 pairs of shoes. They were mainly smaller sizes, so I sent an SOS to a friend of mine in Germany for larger sizes. Within a fortnight she sent me a photograph of herself sitting on 47 banana boxes full of shoes. She had also collected 40 children's winter coats in various sizes, so that finally we had to look for alternative transport to shift the German donations to Romania.

Back at home we did equally well. Both Northern and Southern Ireland were now involved, big firms, small firms and individuals. Shortly, I would have to stop the flow.

In the meantime Douglas had established contact with a surgeon of a large hospital in Bucharest. He urgently needed plaster of Paris, sterile dressings, antibiotics and anaesthetics. The transport of the latter into Romania was forbidden. I had witnessed operations being performed without anaesthetics in Germany at the end of the war and immediately I heard of this restriction I said to Ernest: "We'll take the stuff if we can get it." Connections and interviews with important people had to be exploited. Ernest and I went to Dublin on the train for a private appointment. We returned with a parcel for which I believe we had paid 250 punts in cash. Of course, it was only a drop in the ocean within a country like Romania, but until the health arrangements for the people of that country could be sorted out, it was better than nothing. That parcel would have covered best part of a hundred operations, a donation from a number of surgeons. Our small contribution was but a figure for some records. All other medical supplies we collected from health centres North and South of the border and from chemists. They included 2 hundred-weight of plaster of Paris in the bottom of the trailer, to which was added another half hundred-weight under our seats at a later date. We had two giant bags of milk powder, 2,600 packets of soup, boxes with tins of meat, medication, underwear, you name it - and one teddy.

I had refused any more toys. What had been collected went with another transport. There was no more room in our car and trailer. I only took cash now which could be changed into American dollars and buy most things in Romania. The teddy, which I had fallen in love with, was an exception. It was the right size to be squeezed in under the sunshine roof of the car to protect the glass and it was the most beautiful teddy I had ever seen. I seemed to be unable to leave it behind. Should anyone ask me why I had packed that article in particular when all other toys were left behind for the next transport, I would simply answer that I would need a soft pillow in the tent. 'My' teddy would come.

When the last snow had left Romania, we set off. With our load we hoped to average about 250 miles per day and the time of arrival was based on that assumption. At the end of most days we tried to hire a caravan for the night and keep the load right beside us. If that was impossible we would pitch a tent, readily accessible in the back of the car. In five days' time, at two o'clock in the afternoon local time, we were to meet Douglas at a certain lay-by in the middle of Romania near the town of Sibiu. He would guide us to a safe camp site in the woods for the last night, before reaching Bucharest. By then and in that country our load would be worth a fortune and in Romania worth stealing.

We made good time and drove into an utterly neglected East Germany early on the third day. I was map reading at the time. "If we branch off at the next turning, we would be in Colditz in" I hesitated, trying to convert kilometres into miles, "about 15 miles. Shall we make that detour?" Why not? If we did not take this opportunity, we might never see the infamous castle. Presently he turned off the main road and we saw the castle long before we had reached the village. The latter looked quite dowdy but for a baker's shop, which was clean and bright with lights shining onto its tempting window displays. It could easily have competed with the most modern equivalent in the West.

We stopped in the car park in the middle of the market square, got out, locked up and went for a walk. I was quite interested to learn what the locals knew about the castle. On our way to it I asked a middle-aged woman.

"No idea, you'll have to ask in an old people's home. Wait a minute, someone told me some time ago it was a mental hospital"

The man I asked next seemed to have more time than the woman.

"They look after mentally deranged people there."

"And before that?" I asked. "I heard, it was a prison camp."

"Don't think so. Mind you, they had camps all over the place in those days."

"Sorry I stopped you. I thought perhaps your parents had at some time mentioned the prisoners."

"Why? We had enough worries of our own."

I cleared my throat and enlightened him. "This castle housed captured allied officers for years and you mean to say no-one in Colditz knew about it? They must have been brought there and fed. They must have received letters and parcels – and did all that happen without the Germans being suspicious or curious? I can't believe that. We Germans weren't as stupid or naïve in those days. We would have asked questions even if we kept our mouths shut afterwards."

"No, no, no. If you're talking about the war, here in the East, the prisoners would only have been Soviets and Poles. They weren't allowed in the village. So we let them get on with it, up there." He squinted up at the castle.

My last question was: "Have you lived here all your life?"

"Of course, and so did my parents and grandparents. Should we not have done? It was Germany then and is now."

"Of course," I repeated the start of his last sentence and was none the wiser.

The locals at that time knew absolutely nothing about the history of the castle.

I thanked the stranger and hurried along to catch up with Ernest. It was unbelievable that a community like Colditz could have been kept in ignorance of what went on in their castle. "How could they keep that a secret?" Ernest wondered. Supplies must have been delivered very early or late in the day. A lot of the staff had probably slept on the premises. Military vehicles were in any case seen everywhere at any time. But most important of all, the inhabitants of the village would have been told that if they so much as mentioned the words Colditz Castle they would be enemies of the state and treated accordingly. Maybe out of fear that the Nazis might come to power again or lack of interest after the castle had been emptied of prisoners, they kept quiet because they were preoccupied with their own survival. Like the man had said, during the war there were prison camps all over the place.

Together Ernest and I climbed the hill to the castle. At the entrance gates an official sat in a small hut, checking identities and letting delivery vans pass. Access to the courtyard was forbidden, but when we told him how far we had come we were allowed to go just past the archway to the start of the cobbled courtyard. We saw all the little windows, behind which the prisoners had had their quarters. There were now different souls living within these walls, severely mentally handicapped people. We saw no sign of them. Structurally nothing had changed. To me it was also interesting to note that the people in the village knew who now lived in the castle. Freedom of speech had at last arrived in East Germany. We walked back to the village. It was time we left.

There were still three countries to pass through. We had no trouble with the car or trailer and in the early hours of the fifth day we arrived at the Romanian border. We were in good time to keep the appointment with Douglas at the agreed lay-by.

A female customs officer wanted to see our documents - green cards, visas from the Romanian embassy in London, both in

English and Romanian, a list of what we were carrying in English and Romanian and all stamped by the Romanian Embassy as permissible cargo. What we were carrying illegally with our medical supplies was not listed. At that time in the morning we were the only travellers at the border post.

The officer walked round the car and trailer several times and informed us in sign language that we were short of another form. She asked us to pull in at the side of the road. Outwardly she seemed quite friendly and we soon established that she could speak some French and German as well as her own language. In French and German we tried to find out what form was missing, because we had been most concerned that all formalities were in order. Her answers seemed vague, with even a suggestion that we should go back to London and ask for a particular form number which no-one had ever mentioned before.

In the end she relented by suggesting to check our cargo herself before letting us proceed. To us, conversing in English, there was a big difference between abandoning the trip and letting her search our cargo, but what about the illegal drugs for the hospital? Would she find those? To me, her sudden switch from sending us back to searching our cargo seemed strange. I mistrusted her and Ernest also wondered what she had really wanted. In any case we would now miss our meeting with Douglas and in those days we had no mobile phone, and we believed that he could not have phoned us, anyway. Now, the customs officer had us pull off the road, open up and start lining up our goods on the verge. We slowly started to do as we were told, fuming with anger and frustration. We discussed the matter still further and Ernest suggested that he would go on unpacking, while I should try and find out if anything could change her mind - a sort of woman-to-woman talk.

I walked up to her little hut and unobtrusively watched her deal with the next car approaching from Hungary and heading for

Romania. There was not much to be seen. She took one quick look inside, was handed a little parcel, smiled at the driver and waved him on. Now I had the answer. She could be bribed. I sauntered up to her. We started chatting. I told her that our son was waiting for us in Sibiu. Had she children? Yes, a little girl of four. It was very hard to make ends meet now. She had to work to survive at all. At a suitable moment I excused myself, went to the car and returned with my super-teddy. I held it out to her and said: "It's for your little girl." After a couple of minutes of speechless admiration she hugged and kissed it and I quietly whispered: "Can we go now?" She simply nodded.

"Ernest," I called out, "stop what you are doing and load the trailer again! We can proceed."

"That must have gone well?" he remarked when I had joined him again.

"I'll tell you in the car." I whispered as I started to help him. "I gave her the teddy."

"I know. I saw you. Where else can you bribe a customs official? I ask you."

"I feel a little bit sorry for her," I said. "She can buy very little for the Romanian money she gets and she found a way to feed and look after her family."

Back in Ireland I would have to tell the donor of the teddy what had happened to him. I could honestly say that the teddy had made it possible for us to arrive safely in Bucharest at all with all our gifts and donations. A lovely little black-haired girl would now be cuddling the teddy. I did not mention that I had never met the girl. I just assumed her to be lovely and have black hair. She would hardly have been blond. The donor was pleased with that story and thanked me very much.

Now in Romania we had finished packing up. One last wave at the customs officer, and we slid onto our respective seats. We would still make it in time to Sibiu.

We went past miles and miles of farmland. Apart from its oil reserves, Romania had always been known as the bread basket of Europe. That must have referred to its fertile soil, because the farm implements we saw now were of a by-gone age. Crops had already been sown in the large fields which stretched as far as the horizon. Here and there small groups of labourers were going out to work on the land, each armed with no more than a primitive hoe.

Despite the poverty, it was a beautiful country with a climate that brought warmth and hope for a good harvest. The miles rolled by and we gradually came closer to our *rendezvous* with Douglas. When we approached the lay-by which he had identified and to which he had given us directions, we were within half an hour of the agreed time. Douglas was sitting on a picnic-bench reading a book, the familiar car with its Northern Ireland registration plates, parked right beside him. It was somewhat surreal, but a wonderful feeling of security came over us, as did a genuine feeling of affection – the bond between us despite the miles and months which had recently separated us. We still had to deliver our load to Bucharest, but we were no longer alone if stopped by police or inquisitive locals. By now Douglas spoke fluent Romanian and his presence gave us confidence as we negotiated the traffic of Bucharest.

Our first night in Romania, however, would be spent many miles from the capital and what seemed like light years from civilisation. Douglas had discovered a secluded location in woods beside a small river. He led the way and we pitched our tents hoping that no-one had seen us leave the main road. It was not a question of fearing for your life in these parts but rather of being robbed. A culture of stealing had developed which affected all parts of the community and would be very hard to stamp out, while there was that much poverty. We were undisturbed apart from sounds late in the evening when a wood-cutter made his way past our camp at the end of a day's work. Douglas engaged him in a brief conversation and bade him "Good-night" to allay any suspicion, and he continued on his way. We cooked a delicious evening meal – delicious because we were at peace – and then went to bed. It was a restless night though, punctuated by the noise of wild animals and the ever-present flow of water from the river. We realised how potentially vulnerable we still were. On more than one occasion Douglas and Ernest walked round the site to ensure that all was safe, but found nothing which could disturb us.

Early the following morning we had breakfast, packed up and were on the road. On the outskirts of Bucharest a car with several men inside squeezed itself between our two cars and gestured us to stop. Those were the kind of danger points where you would come to no harm but lose all your belongings. Douglas had seen the incident in his mirror, stopped and returned to confront them in Romanian. We did not know what he said to them, but they got back into their car and drove off.

We finally pulled up at a lock-up garage, which Douglas had rented, and there we left the loaded trailer and the contents of the car, confident that all was secure. We drove to the flat which the family had rented in Bucharest and, as a last gesture of defiance to would-be thieves, removed the windscreen wipers – a routine to which all Bucharest car owners at that time resorted. Even a bridegroom would carry them into the church as a safety measure.

We climbed the steps to the third floor flat and, amidst hugs and kisses, were once more united with our family. We could sit down over a cup of tea, recount our adventures and hear what life had been like for them. Opportunities to share their experiences had been few and we could listen and enjoy a well-deserved rest. We had made it.

The two eldest children were now going to a French school and were nearly as fluent in French as in English. Ann led a heroic life of making do and organising meals and in good time we would experience life in Bucharest ourselves. We had planned to stay for a week and used the time firstly to deliver the medical supplies to the hospital. There, we had the opportunity to meet the consultant who had passed on to Douglas a list of the most urgently needed supplies which might be within our reach. He was overjoyed with what we had brought and took time to show us the conditions in which he worked. He was aware that it was all inadequate but inspired us with his positive approach and hope for the future. To all who had so generously supported the children of Bucharest he said a sincere "Thank you". He helped to unload our medical supplies, each of us pushing a trolley up to the first lift and finally into his store room. We left, feeling richer for having met a truly dedicated man.

We went with Douglas to the building which was used as a night shelter for the street children who lived in the vicinity of the city's main railway station. In the shelter we met some of the children and the Romanian colleagues with whom Douglas worked. One evening we also accompanied him to the railway station, to the metro and to some of the haunts where he knew street children would be found – children for whom there was no room in the shelter, in which every bunk and floor space were occupied. Of course, there were also the children who had long since resigned themselves to a way of life without a roof, but come the morning they would queue up at the shelter for something hot to eat or drink. I shall never forget the little boy who had had his legs bound as a baby so that he would become a more successful beggar in later life.

When it was time to go, we left the trailer with Douglas for use on their return journey to Ireland. We said "Good-bye" conscious that we were all so far from home. "See you back in Ireland," I called, trying to retain my composure. We drove off, this time with the car almost empty and without a trailer. We were hoping to reach the frontier with Hungary before dark, some 300 miles, and not have to spend the night in a country where we did not feel secure. All went well.

We took a different route home, enjoying the journey more as a holiday. The weather was glorious and we had plenty of time, but our thoughts were in Romania and would be for a long time to come.

20.

After all the 'thank you' speeches had been delivered, we settled down to some boating and gardening. During the evenings we looked at photographs or tried to phone the family. "There is still plenty of space in this album," Ernest mused.

"You are not making plans for the next trip, are you?" I could not believe it.

"Well, I would love to see your little garden in Treptow. We could put the folding kayak in the boot and explore the Masuren Lakes in the East of Poland and then spend a couple of weeks at the Baltic until it is blueberry-picking time. On the way back, we could divert to where you had helped to dig infantry and panzer trenches."

I was getting excited now. "And I would love to call at my school in Treptow again with a load of sweets for the children. Most of them don't know what sweets taste like." We burst out laughing. "How about next spring? Will that give us time to make all the preparations for the East?" I added.

"You seem to have decided very quickly where you want to go," Ernest teased me.

"No, you started it," I protested. The argument stopped when he took me in his arms and whispered: "We'll have a great time." He did not have to tell me and that was how the next holiday was conceived.

There were nearly six months to go before the journey would take place, but we always preferred a fairly long spell of looking forward to some pleasurable event. In between doing a lot of reading, we now seemed to have the dining table permanently cluttered up with an atlas and half a dozen maps of Eastern Europe. Was it really so important to have an itinerary typed up as early as that?

Finally, on a lovely spring morning, we were ready to go. The back of the car had been gutted again and was re-loaded to the brim with sweets. I was thankful that there was no trailer this time. What a treat that would be for the children of Trzebiatow. Sweets are not good food for children, but the age-old motto 'A little bit of what you fancy does you good', must also be true. Indeed, it was inevitable that sweets would be available in Poland in the foreseeable future anyway, if not already. There would have been several hundred children at that school and a few hundred-weights of sweets would at least have meant something for everyone. The teachers would see to a just and limited distribution. What else should or could we have taken as a sign of good will? Poland was not Romania. The gift was not meant to be a helping hand, just a treat from one pupil to another, facilitated by us and donated by a few firms.

We crossed the sea from Larne to Scotland and from Hull to Rotterdam. Europe looked more affluent than ever. Would that be the same in the East?

It was sensible to call on Trzebiatow first. Once the sweets had been unloaded, we would get the kayak off the roof into the car. Although we had a tent and sleeping bags with us, we booked into a guest house a couple of times before crossing at Szczecin into Poland. As we had expected, East Germany looked more prosperous than Poland now. The big brother had obviously helped the former. The land was very flat, the verges sandy and vast forests of pine stretched into the distance each side of the road. It made me still feel very much at home, but I wished there was an *Autobahn* in this area. Every few miles a very small village appeared and changed the speed limit. There were now more cars on the road. People very soon spotted a strange car number and waved before we got anywhere near them. Any visitor was welcome.

After just over 100 km we pulled into Trzebiatow and stopped at the school. "Now the language fun will start," I commented as I got out of the car. Ernest was no help with his suggestion. "I'll wait here till you find a few sacks for the sweets."

Inside, a cleaning lady smiled at me and, for a while, I did not know what to say. I do not remember what I did say in the end, but she was obviously more intelligent than I was, put the broom into my hand and disappeared down the corridor. She came back followed by a lady in a navy blue suit and I rightly assumed she was the head-mistress. She took me to her office which she shared with her deputy and (I could not believe it) put the kettle on. At the time I wished Ernest could see me. He was dying for a cup of tea or coffee.

With a few words of French and German the head-mistress knew exactly why I was there, even that I myself had been a pupil at that school. In the meantime the deputy had vanished and was now returning with a gentleman – the P.E. teacher and fluent English speaker. He had spent several years in India where he had learnt the English language with, not surprisingly, an Indian accent. The kettle had boiled and the head-mistress made coffee. She must have sensed me wondering where this rare and valuable commodity had come from because she whispered something to the P.E. teacher who translated. "We had another visitor a few weeks ago, probably one of your class mates. She gave it to us." I had also not forgotten to bring a pound of coffee, took it out of my bag and put it on the table. The ladies were delighted, even the P.E. teacher smiled before leaving the room and returning with Ernest who would after all get his cup of coffee.

It was a multi-language get-together, so friendly and relaxing after a long journey, that Ernest and I often talked about that interlude. It was all hands on deck, when it came to the unloading and took the five of us several trips to the car until it was empty.

The sweets were taken to the staff room and put into an annex under lock and key, until a decision was reached how best to distribute them. What I had not realised was that this particular day was Europe-wide 'The Day of the Child'. So when it was time for us to leave, we were presented with a certificate, thanking us for the generous gifts to the school. While we were having coffee, the art teacher had been alerted to produce the certificate. It was time we left. We got into the car and the staff waved to us outside the school as well as several classes who had slipped out to do the same. Both Ernest and I had really enjoyed that day and there was more to come. I showed him 'our house' and garden, this time without being challenged by a lady wanting coffee. We did a lap of honour round the market square, had a walk along the station platform and then consulted our maps for further directions.

Next, we headed for Mostowo, a little site of holiday homes beside a large lake, and all inside pine woods. We had packs of ready-meals with us and would enjoy the evening sunshine. On the following day we assembled the kayak and paddled the few miles to the nearest small town for some shopping. We enjoyed Mostowo for a few more days, walking through the blueberry woods. We had, of course, misjudged the blueberry season, but the singing and dancing in the recreation hut was a pleasure to listen to and watch and that made up for the missing blueberries and the bluish red picking-fingers.

The Masuren Lakes used to be part of East Prussia, so we were still in former German territory and still found the odd person speaking German. The distance we had thought of paddling was around 200 miles – from one lake to the next via little stretches of rivers or brooks, at times so overgrown that we had to wade beside the kayak to lighten its load. Although we had brought ointments and gloves, the mosquitoes finally made us give up any further journeys in the area. We did so reluctantly, but it would appear that we had chosen the breeding season for our trip, and we knew when to call a halt. Everything was quickly packed up, the kayak put on the roof rack of the car and we set off north to the Baltic Sea. The one good thing was always the weather. We found another holiday home near sheltered waters and had a fantastic holiday. This time we were surrounded by churches and castles dating back to the times of the holy knights.

Towards the end of our stay there, we had spread our maps out again. "To get to what's left of the trenches which I had helped to dig," I began, "we will have to find a place called Pollnow." I only knew the German name. "That town, I remember, was meant to stay on the German side of the trenches. From there we need to travel due east for perhaps a couple of miles, the distance we used to walk to get provisions. At that point the road should pass over a post-war bridge with the trenches running beneath it – like a dry river bed."

"Do you know what," Ernest said, "that ditch will long since have been filled in."

"I doubt it. The Soviet engineers will have put a temporary bridge across to be improved at a later date. Maybe they also breached the ditch, as you call it, but a bridge would have had the facility of a road at each end. I think, we'll find a bridge there." I suddenly realised that Ernest misjudged the extent of the trenches. They will have overgrown, but they won't have disappeared. The Poles had no machinery to tackle such a job, and the Russians had enough problems of their own.

When we arrived in what was Pollnow, there was only one road heading east. Another few minutes and we were there – a post-war bridge – to the left a jungle of overgrown hollows heading northwards and on the right a sloping trench now covered in grass with self-sown trees on both sides. Quite likely it was used for grazing, although I saw no animals. It was as straight as a die and reached as far as the horizon.

"I had no idea," Ernest said, looking over the side. We both stood there, perhaps each having different thoughts. I only remember mine. It had been the middle of summer, our summer holidays. We were working in vests and shorts, the sweat running down our bodies. There were no clothes washing facilities. You simply changed into your spare underwear and hung the wet stuff over a bush. I had been told to keep a first aid sack. In it there were a couple of thousand aspirins and rolls of plaster, already rendered useless with the heat. Whoever had forgotten to bring toilet requirements did without those essentials. The barn nearby was the hospital, where people lay on straw. There was no doctor or nurse and there were neither medical instruments nor medication.

Why should that have upset me now? Hitler had promised us TOTAL WAR. By the time we dug those trenches he had already abandoned us. We were grovelling in dirt and dust for no purpose. He knew it, but we did not die like he had hoped we would. He believed that if he must die then so must the German people. They had not passed the test which destiny had set them. How wrong he was.

We took a few photographs, turned the car round and headed for home. "Never saw any signs of the infantry trench," Ernest mused. "It must have collapsed." Still absorbed with what we had seen, I said: "Probably." That was our last trip to the East. We would have gone again, but age started to impose limits on our journeys.

Sometimes all the planning is of no use because you are simply confronted with problems beyond your control. By the time we had reached West Germany on our return journey I started to feel unwell. We discussed whether to consult a doctor, but I decided against it because I was convinced I had eaten something which disagreed with me. Ernest drove faster than usual to Rotterdam and onto the ferry. He put me to bed in the cabin. I was shivering slightly but was much better lying down. Towards morning I was confused but had a normal temperature. We had a few hours drive and another crossing in front of us which we managed in record time. My temperature had gone up again. There was still a long drive ahead of us before we could call at our doctor's surgery. Tired as Ernest was, he had to drive me straight to hospital, another thirty odd miles, where I had my appendix removed that same night. It probably had not been wise to travel home for the operation, but as usual I was lucky.

21.

However useless the trenches had turned out to be, considering the effort that was put into the project, a much more rewarding transformation had taken place in Berlin. It took much longer (roughly ten years) and started shortly after the end of the war. Exact dates would not be available because the idea had only slowly gathered momentum. It was an idea which had to be tackled and which had to be supported by the Soviet occupying forces and by the Western Allies. Berlin had to be rebuilt and before that it had to be cleared of its rubble.

I was in Germany at the beginning of this gigantic undertaking and also followed its progress later from England and Northern Ireland. A dear friend of mine in Düsseldorf kept sending me black and white photographs from a Berlin source with her comments which kept me spell-bound. I suppose those pictures of rubble covering half the city awakened memories of my long walk to fetch my mother and Eka to the West. In my mind I saw the mountains of rubble again, drank the hot potato soup and slept in the bed of the mouth-organ player. Those people whom I had met at that time had cleared up the city. They were the *Trümmerfrauen* (rubble women). "Three cheers for the *Trümmerfrauen*- - - !" I will henceforth refer to them by their German name because the sentiments of admiration which that word conveys would get lost in the translation. I felt for them and I felt I was a part of them. I thought about them regularly and therefore I feel that if the stories of those events had preoccupied me to that extent, then they deserve a place in my autobiography.

Husbands and sons had either fallen in the war or were still prisoners of war. Admittedly, some men had returned to the city and there were older men and teenagers, but the driving force were the women, now the large majority, tackling all aspects of heavy work and planning. There were also serious accidents with loss of life. This was only to be expected when unsafe facades and other masonry had to be brought down. Eventually, tram lines were relocated and small engines and tipping trucks brought to Berlin. Dumping sites were selected in parks, canals, small lakes and on large bomb sites. Then the real work began. Food was short and foot-wear was inadequate, at times just a piece of sack cloth wound round their feet, but the women had hope, enough hope to chip away old cement from wholesome bricks for re-use on new homes. When that time came and when the *Trümmerfrauen* at last lived in those newly built dream apartments, they would remember the hole in the ground through which they had crawled to get to a cellar-bedroom without any privacy and without heat in the winter.

By 1959 the last heap of rubble had been shifted, over 70 million cubic metres in all. Over 600 million bricks are said to have been cleaned for re-use. The above figures, which different residents from Berlin quoted to me, vary only slightly. They are, in any case, not important, except to convey a picture of the enormity of the undertaking. Today's visitors to Berlin may find a monument here and there commemorating the work of the *Trümmerfrauen*, some of which are in parks newly created and landscaped on huge heaps of rubble.

On one of my more recent brief visits to Berlin I sat beside one of those ladies who helped to transform the German capital all those years ago. We were both old now, one a rubble train driver on the Berlin tram lines and the other a trench digger from Germany's border with Poland. On that day we were both travelling on the city's electric train and, as it happened, we both left the train at the same station and headed for the same park, the *Friedrichshain*. I knew it well from my childhood and had read about its transformation and she had spent the best years of her life transforming it. Now, she regarded the place worth visiting and relaxing there and I found that concept very rewarding. We spent a very pleasant afternoon together, chatting about those days when we lived quite close to each other and yet had never met.

The entrance to the park had changed very little. There were still all those fairytale pictures carved in concrete on the low walls each side of the path – Snow-white, Red-riding-hood and all their friends and enemies, but there any similarities to bye-gone days ceased. The park was now vast, built on a thick layer of rubble with two distinct mountains. Underneath those were buried the war-time flak bunkers, the anti-aircraft defence system and search lights, so dreaded by allied bombers. Soviet attempts to bring down these monstrosities after the war had failed and so the two bunkers in question were buried where they stood.

In the meantime we had found a seat. It had been quite a long walk from the station. Now we could admire nature on rubble at leisure. My companion began. "First of all we filled the offices and store rooms of the bunkers below ground with rubble and then the outsides were built up. All this had been a moonscape after the war. A bit further up the mountain I had my accident." It would appear one of the tram rails had subsided and engine and tipping trucks had turned on their sides and slid down the embankment. The trucks had to be emptied with shovels, righted and repaired. Three weeks' time and work were lost. "I'm only telling you this because at times we cried our hearts out because we thought we had taken on too much."

"Tell me," I said, "was it obligatory to become a *Trümmerfrau* after the war? I mean did you all have to do this horrible work?"

"I think you could have refused," she answered after a considerable time, "but we didn't. After all, it was our idea and besides, we were given *Schwerarbeiter* ration cards (heavy worker's ration cards).

That explained a lot. Some would have joined because there would have been extra food, not just for patriotic reasons. I thought my companion was very honest. I knew food was extremely short in those days. They would have worked very hard for the extra loaf and there was no shame attached to that. My companion had the last word. "There were those commentators who proclaimed that we worked for useless *Pfennigs* out of patriotism only. We were hungry and we don't want to be glorified now. Of course, patriotism came into it as well, but that was not the only reason for nearly killing ourselves. Apart from that we also felt it was time we emerged from our holes and cellars in the ground and lived like human beings."

This brought back memories of leading my mother and Eka through Berlin's landscape of destruction. I still cannot believe that there was no mechanical equipment and that some young lads swung from ropes on facades, dismantling high walls which were unsafe. "What are you thinking about?" asked my companion when she saw me gazing into space and I told her about bringing my mother and sister to West Germany. Her comment did not surprise me.

"You don't know how lucky you were. Your journey from Berlin to Lüneburg was a once-off thing because the Russians soon discovered that their arrangements were being abused, that they needed German speaking guards and prison vans as stand-by. You would never have made it a week later. You would never have made it at all. There were already plans discussed to seal the whole of West Berlin off, build a wall if necessary, defend it and do the same with the East/West German frontier. You managed it and that in record time. Let me tell you, your guardian angel must have been right beside you all the way."

"I know that," I replied. "Sometimes it is good to be young and not think too much about consequences. I never gave that aspect any thought at that time. I don't even remember having ever thought about it since. It had to be done, a bit like you clearing up the rubble. Perhaps I should have made more detailed preparations, but there were too many unknown factors to consider."

We left our seat after a while and walked towards the 'mountains'. The whole area was wooded now with sophisticated play-areas for children and there was no shortage of them. Presently I stopped to admire the view from a height, little Berlin down below. The area had always been as flat as a pancake. Now I could easily imagine that I was on a climbing expedition, a coil of rope on my back instead of a little rucksack and a handful of spikes hanging from my belt instead of my small purse. I suppose the big blocks of flats in the distance gave the game away.

"How did you get up to this level with your loads of rubble?" I asked. "The level was continuously built up with old timber shoring the sides so that we could tip over the edges, but it had to be done properly."

The little park of yesterday had now all the trimmings of a national park. The covering of three metres of top soil was enough to sustain mature trees and I was quite sorry to leave. I had now seen three mountains and one mountain-range in Berlin and wondered how many there were altogether. Even the little train driver beside me could not answer that question. We walked back to the station where we parted company. She went home on the bus and I waited for the electric train.

22.

About ten years before Ernest was due to retire his firm closed its branch in Castledawdson. He was offered alternative employment in Croydon, but by that time we were not interested in taking up the offer. He loved his home in Ireland and I was happy as a music teacher. Neither of us wanted to move to England at this late stage. We had built our bungalow in Castledawson. That could hardly be matched in Croydon and we were past wanting promotion where our jobs were concerned. We also knew that there would be no jobs on offer near our home comparable with his present position. I volunteered to give up my job. Maybe I would find employment in England, but he had set his mind on staying in Castledawson, on working his little patch and landscaping more and more of the ground which still had to be cleared. He would find some job he assured me or retire early and he did try his luck in some small provincial office a few miles away, but I could see that would not work.

I cannot remember whose idea it was, but it could have been mine, at least it sounds like me. If he was so keen to work on his land as an antidote to clerical work, why not start a garden centre? I was certainly very interested in such a project. I would support him and help him at times. He could get a stack of books out of the library and go to horticultural courses. I would gladly be the bread winner until he had established the business. Such a solution had never occurred to either of us. For once he would spend the rest of his working life doing something he really loved and that would be our problem solved. Success would only come with hard work and he was not afraid of that. He studied and toiled from morning till night. There was much to learn which no book could tell you, but he just loved the idea of running his own business and that mainly outdoors.

I was always a keen gardener and now, I simply added another interest to my collection of hobbies – horticulture. It was time I stopped my painting of landscapes for a while and helped to design the layout of the garden centre.

He quickly learned that stock had to be propagated by him and not bought in, at least much of it, if he wanted to make a profit. What had been propagated had also to be grown on until it was fit for sale. In other words, he would not be earning much initially; thank goodness I was, so that was no problem. Three 60-foot tunnels went up and two glasshouses. Our bricklayer was busy building walls for display areas and eventually the sign went up at the entrance gate and we were open for business. We both knew it would take time to establish the business, but I can honestly say we made a success of it, because it was also an antidote for me to be out in the fresh air and talk to people after a day's teaching. When I retired from teaching I could help even more.

I had started writing long before my retirement from teaching. It started off with a few articles and gradually developed into short stories, which I then sent away to a company of experts for correction and criticism. I was not impressed by their replies. My work was judged by numbers one to five which I found insufficient. For a while I lost interest. Then, quite by chance, I befriended a part-time lecturer at Queen's University who wanted to help me. She was extremely detailed in her assessment, and there developed a kind of correspondence course, always related to just a few pages of writing. Those were no longer recognizable when she had finished correcting them. I think I made very good progress under her tuition and she felt the same. Subjects under discussion varied, but were usually connected with some of my experiences. I did not seem able to shake them off.

Suddenly the lady died. It was a big shock to me and I stopped writing altogether. Years later I picked up the interest once more, wrote a couple of books about animals and Ireland in German and had them published in Germany. I had published four novels in England, all in English reflecting my own experiences, but I was never really happy with any of them. It took another period of research, before my publisher in England suggested I should write my autobiography. That turned out to be another drawn-out effort which had all the signs of never being completed. This time external circumstances prevented me from completing the work.

We had latterly moved to the Donegal area, where we had spent many happy holidays and on the shores of Lough Melvin we had finally built our dream house. Initially we were not too far away from the family and visited each other regularly, but we were getting old and things would not remain as they were. The boats were sold off – one by one, and at some stage I developed severe pains in both my knees. I was lying in the back of the car and Ernest drove me from one hospital to another, from one consultant to another, both north and south of the border. I was diagnosed as suffering from half a dozen different ailments. No medication was of any help. The pain persisted. I could not walk and imagined spending the rest of my life in a wheelchair.

A consultant from Galway came up with the correct diagnosis, after he talked to me on and off for a couple of hours. He quizzed me about every smallest incident, injury and unusual happening during the past few years and then simply said: "You have been bitten by a tick. It has destroyed your cartilage in both knees completely. The knees have to be replaced." He was right. I had the operations in Sligo General Hospital and never looked back. Determined to walk again, I exercised the legs from day two of each operation and later walked for miles on crutches - daily - rain or shine. Now, at 87, I walk unaided and cycle, if not far, then regularly and I would say my heart will certainly curb my efforts long before my knees will. In those days everyone was very kind to me, the family covered long distances to be with me. They supported Ernest, and things looked very bright again.

Not so long after my ordeal, it was Ernest's turn. He suffered an aneurysm one afternoon. It was a miracle that he recovered, but he only lived for another two years, often falling and hurting himself. I was pleased that I could now look after him. Eventually, he had to go into hospital where, after a few months, he died of cancer.

23.

The support of my family was magnificent. Both Douglas and I were at his bedside when he died. He was cremated in Belfast and his ashes were buried at sea off the Donegal coast, again with family and friends round me and at a moving private ceremony. It will be a lasting memory and it will always be part of me.

In those early days after his death I just could not imagine arriving home in future without anyone ever opening the door and greeting me, that I would only ever cook a meal for myself although I did not care whether I lived or died. It was the loss of hope that some day things would be normal again, that we would live together again which I found so hard to bear. There was only one place where we might see each other again and I could hardly wait to get there myself.

These were first reactions, of course, because deep down I knew that millions of people had lost loved ones and were living alone. Now, at least, I knew how they had felt.

This may be the shortest chapter of the book, but only because words can no longer describe my feelings.

24.

I stayed with Douglas and Ann for a while and then returned to our bungalow. I walked through every room, hoping to find someone, hoping to get an answer when I called out, but there was neither a moving image nor a sound. Not even the clock was ticking because the batteries should have been replaced a couple of months ago.

The nearest neighbour lived half a mile away. The two houses nearest to me were only holiday homes. I could not stay here. I could not live here on my own. Every time the wind brought a twig or branch down I would think some person was trying to unlock the front or back door. I switched the kitchen light on and immediately turned it off again for fear someone, hiding in the bushes, would see me.

At the end of the road lived a couple which I knew reasonably well. They had recently moved there from the North. I picked up the phone. "Can I please sleep in your house tonight and would you fetch me?"

"Be there in a minute!" a Belfast voice answered and I sighed with relief. People were so very kind. My reaction to Ernest's death was so strange that I feared I would go out of my mind. After all, it was not the first time that I found myself alone in the house. Ernest's long stays in hospital saw to that and I had ample warning that any time soon he would pass away. Not so long ago I had taken a few days' break to visit my sister, but what I needed was a few weeks' rest.

The question of where should I live worried me again. The present home was too remote for me, particularly if I could no longer drive. There was no bus stop in the immediate area. The bungalow was also too big and, sitting on nearly four acres of land, I would be marooned if a tree fell across the drive. I wondered why the thought of moving into a smaller house or apartment had not occurred to us earlier; it had to Douglas and Ann but not to us. Suddenly it was too late.

After much deliberation, I put the house on the market and moved to Germany to live near Eka. I would live there in the Black Forest, in a nice climate, until I had found my old self again or even longer. Eka and I were on our own now, would support each other and maybe even move into an old peoples' home together, one day.

Ernest had miscalculated the events at the end of his life, for he died in hospital and not in his bed. Now, I was making the same mistake in a slightly different form. Having lived and worked in Ireland for over 50 years, I was probably no longer German, if one discounts the accident of birth. Germany did not feel like home - not anymore. Bricks and mortar, a nice climate, the lovely smell of pines, they were fine when on holiday, but they were not essential for a home. Home is where I spent my working life, where I was happily married and where my family lives now. At least I got that one sorted out before it would be too late again.

Bad Wildbad (Bad translates into spa) is a small town with thermal springs and with one of the largest natural parks in southwest Germany. Through the park races a little boulder-strewn river, always busy, carrying winter snow, spring debris, or autumn leaves. In the old days it was used for ferrying timber from the mountains to the valleys and the British aristocracy had regularly turned up there for their holidays. They had loved this wonderful spot and were only short of one thing – their Anglican Church. That was soon rectified. The English paid for a small church to be built in the middle of this German park. Today it is still there, well maintained and regularly used for weddings. Several signposts point in its direction – "To the

English Church". It was after the Second World War that Britain relinquished the building which was now in urgent need of repair. It had served its purpose. The Germans restored it and kept its English name.

My thoughts were still with Ernest. I had kept a little carton filled with his ashes for company and rightly or wrongly I think it made me feel more settled. That, phone calls to the family, Eka's occasional company and the business of settling in had given me peace of mind again. I feared it might not last long, but it had the effect of healing recent wounds. I had often wondered what to do with the ashes eventually. Suddenly I knew.

Very early one morning I put the carton into my saddle bag, tied my beloved spade across the handlebars and cycled to a park bench near the English church. At the rear entrance of the church I cut a square of turf out of the lawn and emptied the remaining ashes into a little hole. All was replaced and covered up, a few bulbs and forget-me-nots planted and I bowed my head in prayer. No-one had seen me trespassing in that way and I was proud of my morning's work. Ernest and I were still together in Bad Wildbad. I cycled past the church every day and would call out "Hallo, Dear" as I passed. I would often sit on the nearby bench reading, when I had finished my shopping. In the winter the little grave would always be covered with snow. The rest of the time the park gardeners would mow over it once a month. In the spring the bulbs would push their green spikes through the short grass and the previous year's seeds of forget-me-nots, which had escaped the blades of the mowers, would germinate. Last time I watched, I saw the gardeners leave the forget-me-nots blooming and not cut them down. I call that progress, because now they have an Englishman keeping an eye on his church again.

Friendly neighbours, contact with my sister and visits from my family kept me busy. Healthy exercise restored my confidence.

I could be pleased with my progress. So often in my life I was at the end of my strength. I felt I had enough of it and could take no more and then I got back on my feet and brushed myself off, as if nothing had happened. Time and time again I vowed I would avoid certain pitfalls in future, but that was easier said than done. I am grateful that I always clambered out of misery back into happiness again.

In the spring of 2012, early in April, I moved back to Northern Ireland. I enjoy having the family round me, having delightful friends and I have, I believe, at last learnt to be still busy and happy. There will be no further bouncing going on in my life, not in any direction.

People who knew me, often felt sorry for me, having wasted my time and effort on two such moves with a lot of my belongings and at my age. To that I can only say that I had to sample the life in Germany once more, before I knew where I now belonged. No time was wasted. I will always love Germany, but my home is now in Ireland. The family had to come first and precious few of them are left in Germany. I was always delighted when, on my travels in Germany, I found something which I recognised. It was the old building, the old spirit and the old environment which I was looking for. I did not want to forget any part of it, good or bad so that I could learn from it or revel in it, and I was delighted that a better Germany had emerged from the ashes of the Hitler period. It was a satisfaction which I appreciated enormously no matter where I lived.

⚜ ⚜ ⚜

I live beside the sea now, looking out onto a harbour and watching sailing boats coming and going just like Ernest and I had done so many times in our lives. In those days we had frequented a different part of the Irish coast, but the charm of the people and the beauty of the coastline were very similar. That feeling of having finally settled down did not preclude me from planning a holiday with Eka in the Black Forest again. During her visit to Carrickfergus in 2012 we discussed the possibility of spending some time as tourists in Bad Wildbad. Arrangements were made and in May 2013 we both arrived back in my old stamping ground and had a lovely holiday.

When she left to go home, I stayed on a bit longer. I had several friends to visit and I had the urge to be on my own for the last few days. I visited the place where I had left some of Ernest's ashes and turned a little problem over in my mind. I enjoyed sitting on that park bench beside the English church which was so familiar to me. However, the little problem would not go away, not that day nor the day after. Six or seven years ago I had lost my wedding ring in Ireland on a caravan holiday. At that time Ernest did not mind whether I replaced the ring or not, but I felt bare without it. We made plans to buy another one, but there was always something more important to attend to and in time, I began to wonder whether the whole procedure was necessary at my age. It was necessary, I told myself now and I got up and walked purposefully to the main street of Bad Wildbad.

I bought a wedding ring the right size, went back to the park and to Ernest's little grave beside the English church. I put the new ring on the little mound of grass and asked the Lord to bless it. There was no one present to put it on my finger, to hug me or to kiss me. So I simply wiped away the tears, picked up the ring and put it on my finger. A warm feeling engulfed me as though I was in someone's arms. It felt like being married all over again and I now had proof that true love is eternal.

POSTSCRIPT

F urther to the beginning of this book where I described how my father tried to find out more about our ancestors on his side of the family, it was the foreign name of the first John Schiel which had puzzled him. However, he had to be satisfied with the facts that this distant relative was a seafarer based in the former Baltic Port of Memel like all the other John Schiels of his family. It also meant that this stranger would almost certainly have been an immigrant to the area from the British Isles or Ireland.

I now know that the surname in question was probably Shiell or even Sheil, quite common in Scotland and Ireland, before it was Germanized to Schiel in the case of new settlers in Memel. A couple of hundred years ago family names and place names were passed on by way of mouth, hence the difference in spellings.

For a long time I thought that my investigations would lead me no further, but in the age of the computer everything is possible. I found out from the internet that Memel had been a very busy German Baltic port shipping timber, but also salt and sugar (made from sugar beet) on a regular basis to Ballyshannon in Donegal, Ireland. The main return cargo was whiskey and also wool. How very convenient that the distillery stood right on the quayside. Indeed, it was probably built there to facilitate the Irish trade with Germany and Norway.

The boats often had a mixed crew of Irish and German sailors of whom at least one Irish sailor had settled in Memel and now spelt his surname *Schiel*. All the different versions of the name were listed in the internet and I now thought it very likely that my ancestors on my father's side originally came from the area around Ballyshannon. There was even a first mate by the name of Schiel on a crew list. The German authorities in Memel never understood where these sailors were born and the applicants could not spell the place name in German. So the answer to that question remained blank on the Schiel page of the archive records. Therefore, I cannot be 100% sure of all the facts, but all of them point to the strong possibility that something in me, or of me, or in my genes is unmistakably Irish.

All my discoveries were food for thought as I closed down the computer and started making preparations for my holiday in Donegal. This time I really looked forward to my trip to Ballyshannon. It had been planned for a long time because I had many friends there and loved the area. On arrival Beatrice met me at the bus stop and we headed straight for the coffee shop which was so familiar to us. There was much excitement because we had much to talk about. I told her that it looked as though some of my ancestors may have come from Ballyshannon. She nearly fell off the chair while I relaxed after my long bus journey, but I could see that her mind was working overtime. Presently she had it all worked out. We would first go to the museum which had been set up in the same building as our coffee shop. I remembered when Ernest was cared for by Beatrice in hospital, he had often told me that you did not argue with Beatrice. Her command was always to be obeyed. Bearing that in mind, I now followed her upstairs without demur. Indeed, I was delighted to have found a guide in my search for hereditary clues.

The little museum had quite a good display of books, pictures and other memorabilia, for such a small town. One could sense that there was an active interest in keeping the past alive, an interest in what historic facts had been remembered or recorded by relatives and neighbours. We were, after all, in a land where everyone knew everyone else. We were in the oldest town in Ireland. Before putting any questions to the chairperson we walked round the room. Suddenly I stopped and stared at a picture on the wall. It showed three old sailing vessels moored in Ballyshannon harbour and I felt sure I had seen that picture before in our flat in Berlin. Only there the boats had been moored in the Memel harbour. My father had brought the picture back from one of his trips to Memel and I vaguely remembered the occasion. Now, I saw the picture of the boats again, this time in Irish waters.

I made a few purchases in the museum which included a certain picture on the wall. Meanwhile Beatrice had made an appointment with the local historian and she drove me to his address. We talked for a long time. It would appear that I was the first person he had met who had connections with their Memel trading post and as such he was interested in all I had to say on the subject. He told me of a case where a Ballyshannon lady had settled in Trondheim, Norway, in the 19th century. Her Irish roots had been discovered by the local historian, who was now sitting beside me, and by a researcher in Norway. All my Irish roots may also come to light one day, for what we now need to know is where exactly our first John Shiel was born and in what year, before he migrated to Memel on one of the timber boats. I am keeping in touch with the local historian and the chairperson of the museum while the hunt is on for that old lady or gentleman who knew someone who had kept records of a young lad, probably called John Shiel. He may well have been a substitute for a sick sailor on the whiskey run to Memel. Alternatively, church records might reveal that a young man by that name had left Ireland from Ballyshannon in the second half of the 18th century and that he never returned to live in his homeland permanently, for our family had proof in Berlin that, when not at sea, he lived and finally died in Memel.

So, it would appear that the spirit of "John the First" had come to me in my old age, to keep me company, as I remember my past and he might yet drop a hint where to locate proof of his identity.